AF433531

55 Indian
Recipes for Home

By: Kelly Johnson

Table of Contents

- Sambar
- Baingan Ka Bharta
- Tandoori Fish
- Chicken Do Pyaza
- Gobi Manchurian
- Rajasthani Dal Baati
- Chole Bhature
- Chicken Chettinad
- Kathi Roll
- Chicken Sukka
- Mutton Curry
- Tomato Rasam
- Dosa
- Achari Chicken
- Kheema Pav
- Chicken Handi
- Bhel Puri
- Methi Chicken
- Kadhi Pakora
- Prawn Curry

Butter Chicken

Ingredients:

For Marination:

- 500g boneless chicken, cut into cubes
- 1 cup plain yogurt
- 1 tablespoon ginger-garlic paste
- 1 teaspoon red chili powder
- 1 teaspoon turmeric powder
- 1 teaspoon garam masala
- Salt to taste

For the Curry:

- 2 tablespoons butter
- 1 tablespoon oil
- 1 large onion, finely chopped
- 2 teaspoons ginger-garlic paste
- 1 teaspoon cumin powder
- 1 teaspoon coriander powder
- 1 teaspoon red chili powder (adjust to taste)
- 1 cup tomato puree
- 1/2 cup cashew nuts (soaked in warm water for 15 minutes)
- 1 cup heavy cream
- 1 teaspoon garam masala
- Salt to taste
- Fresh coriander leaves for garnish

Instructions:

In a bowl, mix together all the marination ingredients and let the chicken marinate for at least 2 hours or overnight in the refrigerator.

Heat oil and butter in a pan. Add chopped onions and sauté until golden brown.

Add ginger-garlic paste and sauté for another minute until the raw smell disappears.

Add cumin powder, coriander powder, and red chili powder. Cook for a couple of minutes.

Add tomato puree and cook until the oil separates from the masala.
Meanwhile, blend the soaked cashew nuts into a smooth paste using a little water.
Add the marinated chicken to the pan and cook until it's no longer pink.
Stir in the cashew paste and let it cook for a few minutes.
Pour in the heavy cream, garam masala, and salt. Simmer for about 10-15 minutes until the chicken is cooked through and the curry thickens.
Garnish with fresh coriander leaves and serve hot with naan or rice.

Enjoy your delicious Butter Chicken!

Chicken Biryani

Ingredients:

For Marination:

- 500g chicken, cut into pieces
- 1 cup yogurt
- 1 tablespoon ginger-garlic paste
- 1 teaspoon red chili powder
- 1/2 teaspoon turmeric powder
- 1 teaspoon garam masala
- Salt to taste

For Rice:

- 2 cups basmati rice, soaked for 30 minutes and drained
- 4 cups water
- 1 bay leaf
- 4-5 whole cloves
- 4-5 whole green cardamom
- 1 cinnamon stick
- Salt to taste

For Biryani Masala:

- 2 large onions, thinly sliced
- 2 tomatoes, chopped
- 1/2 cup chopped coriander leaves
- 1/2 cup chopped mint leaves
- 4 tablespoons ghee or oil
- 1 teaspoon cumin seeds
- 2 teaspoons biryani masala powder
- 1/2 teaspoon red chili powder
- Salt to taste

Instructions:

Marinate the chicken with yogurt, ginger-garlic paste, red chili powder, turmeric powder, garam masala, and salt. Let it marinate for at least 1-2 hours.

In a large pot, bring water to a boil. Add soaked and drained basmati rice, bay leaf, cloves, cardamom, cinnamon, and salt. Cook the rice until it is 70-80% cooked. Drain the water and set aside.
In a separate pan, heat ghee or oil. Add cumin seeds and sliced onions. Sauté until the onions turn golden brown.
Add chopped tomatoes and cook until they become soft.
Add biryani masala powder, red chili powder, and salt. Cook the masala until the oil separates from it.
Add marinated chicken pieces and cook until the chicken is partially cooked.
In a large heavy-bottomed pan or biryani pot, layer half of the partially cooked rice at the bottom.
Spread the partially cooked chicken masala over the rice.
Sprinkle chopped coriander leaves and mint leaves over the chicken layer.
Layer the remaining rice over the chicken masala.
Drizzle some ghee over the top layer of rice and sprinkle biryani masala powder.
Cover the pot with a tight-fitting lid or seal with aluminum foil. Cook on low heat for about 20-25 minutes until the chicken is fully cooked and the rice is tender.
Gently fluff the biryani with a fork, mixing the layers.

Serve the Chicken Biryani hot with raita or a side salad. Enjoy your delicious and aromatic Chicken Biryani!

Paneer Tikka

Ingredients:

- 250g paneer, cut into cubes
- 1 cup thick yogurt
- 2 tablespoons ginger-garlic paste
- 1 tablespoon red chili powder
- 1 teaspoon turmeric powder
- 1 teaspoon cumin powder
- 1 teaspoon coriander powder
- 1 teaspoon garam masala
- 1 tablespoon lemon juice
- Salt to taste
- 2 tablespoons vegetable oil
- Skewers (wooden or metal)

For Garnish:

- Chopped coriander leaves
- Lemon wedges

Instructions:

In a bowl, mix yogurt, ginger-garlic paste, red chili powder, turmeric powder, cumin powder, coriander powder, garam masala, lemon juice, salt, and vegetable oil to make the marinade.

Add the paneer cubes to the marinade, making sure each piece is well-coated.

Cover the bowl and let it marinate in the refrigerator for at least 2 hours, or preferably overnight for better flavor.

If you're using wooden skewers, soak them in water for about 30 minutes to prevent them from burning during grilling.

Preheat your grill or oven to a medium-high heat.

Thread the marinated paneer cubes onto skewers.

Grill the skewers for about 10-15 minutes, turning occasionally until the paneer is cooked and has a slight char on the edges. If using an oven, you can bake them at around 200°C (400°F) for 15-20 minutes.

Once done, garnish with chopped coriander leaves and serve hot with lemon wedges.

Paneer Tikka can be enjoyed on its own or with mint chutney and a side of salad. It also makes a great party appetizer. Enjoy your delicious Paneer Tikka!

Aloo Gobi

Ingredients:

- 1 medium-sized cauliflower, cut into florets
- 3 medium-sized potatoes, peeled and cubed
- 2 tablespoons vegetable oil
- 1 teaspoon cumin seeds
- 1 onion, finely chopped
- 2 tomatoes, chopped
- 1 tablespoon ginger-garlic paste
- 1/2 teaspoon turmeric powder
- 1 teaspoon red chili powder (adjust to taste)
- 1 teaspoon cumin powder
- 1 teaspoon coriander powder
- Salt to taste
- 1/2 teaspoon garam masala
- Fresh coriander leaves for garnish

Instructions:

Heat oil in a large pan over medium heat. Add cumin seeds and let them splutter.
Add chopped onions and sauté until they turn golden brown.
Add ginger-garlic paste and sauté for a minute until the raw smell disappears.
Add chopped tomatoes and cook until they become soft and the oil starts to separate from the mixture.
Add turmeric powder, red chili powder, cumin powder, coriander powder, and salt. Mix well.
Add potato cubes and cauliflower florets to the pan. Mix them with the spice mixture until they are well coated.
Cover the pan and let the vegetables cook on low to medium heat, stirring occasionally. You may need to add a little water if the mixture is sticking to the bottom.
Cook until the potatoes and cauliflower are tender. This may take about 15-20 minutes.
Once the vegetables are cooked, add garam masala and mix well.
Garnish with fresh coriander leaves.

Serve Aloo Gobi hot with naan, roti, or rice. It makes a delicious and wholesome vegetarian dish. Enjoy!

Tandoori Chicken

Ingredients:

For Marination:

- 1.5 kg chicken pieces (drumsticks, thighs, or a mix)
- 1 cup plain yogurt
- 2 tablespoons ginger-garlic paste
- 1 tablespoon red chili powder
- 1 tablespoon ground coriander
- 1 tablespoon ground cumin
- 1 teaspoon turmeric powder
- 1 teaspoon garam masala
- 1 teaspoon smoked paprika (for color, optional)
- 2 tablespoons lemon juice
- Salt to taste
- 2 tablespoons vegetable oil

For Garnish:

- Fresh coriander leaves
- Lemon wedges

Instructions:

In a large bowl, mix together yogurt, ginger-garlic paste, red chili powder, ground coriander, ground cumin, turmeric powder, garam masala, smoked paprika (if using), lemon juice, salt, and vegetable oil to make the marinade.
Make deep cuts on the chicken pieces to allow the marinade to penetrate.
Coat the chicken pieces with the marinade, making sure each piece is well-covered. Cover the bowl and let it marinate in the refrigerator for at least 4 hours or preferably overnight for better flavor.
Preheat your oven to the highest temperature setting (usually around 475°F or 245°C).
If using a grill, preheat it to medium-high heat.

Thread the marinated chicken pieces onto skewers if you're using the oven. If using a grill, you can directly place them on the grill grates.
Place the skewers on a baking sheet or grill and cook in the preheated oven or grill for about 20-25 minutes or until the chicken is cooked through and has a nice char on the edges.
Garnish with fresh coriander leaves and serve hot with lemon wedges.

Tandoori Chicken is often served with mint chutney or raita. Enjoy the smoky and

flavorful taste of this classic Indian dish!

Palak Paneer

Ingredients:

- 250g paneer, cut into cubes
- 500g fresh spinach leaves, washed and chopped
- 1 large onion, finely chopped
- 2 tomatoes, chopped
- 2 green chilies, chopped (adjust to taste)
- 1 tablespoon ginger-garlic paste
- 1 teaspoon cumin seeds
- 1 teaspoon garam masala
- 1/2 teaspoon turmeric powder
- 1 teaspoon coriander powder
- 1/2 teaspoon red chili powder (adjust to taste)
- Salt to taste
- 2 tablespoons oil or ghee
- 2 tablespoons cream (optional, for garnish)

Instructions:

Blanch the spinach: Bring a pot of water to boil. Add the chopped spinach leaves and cook for about 2 minutes. Drain the spinach and immediately transfer it to a bowl of ice water to retain its green color. Once cooled, blend the spinach into a smooth puree.

Heat oil or ghee in a pan over medium heat. Add cumin seeds and let them splutter.

Add finely chopped onions and sauté until they become golden brown.

Add ginger-garlic paste and chopped green chilies. Sauté for a minute until the raw smell disappears.

Add chopped tomatoes and cook until they become soft and the oil separates from the mixture.

Add turmeric powder, coriander powder, red chili powder, and salt. Mix well.

Add the spinach puree to the pan and cook for 5-7 minutes, allowing the flavors to blend.

Add garam masala and mix well.

Add the paneer cubes and cook for an additional 5 minutes until the paneer absorbs the flavors of the spinach.

If the consistency is too thick, you can add a little water to achieve your desired consistency.
Optionally, swirl in cream for added richness and garnish.

Serve Palak Paneer hot with naan, roti, or rice. It's a nutritious and delicious dish that's loved by many. Enjoy!

Rogan Josh

Ingredients:

- 500g boneless lamb, cut into cubes
- 3 tablespoons vegetable oil or ghee
- 2 large onions, finely chopped
- 2 tomatoes, chopped
- 1/4 cup plain yogurt
- 1 tablespoon ginger-garlic paste
- 2 teaspoons ground coriander
- 2 teaspoons ground cumin
- 1 teaspoon turmeric powder
- 1 teaspoon red chili powder (adjust to taste)
- 1 teaspoon paprika (for color, optional)
- 1 teaspoon garam masala
- Salt to taste
- 1 cinnamon stick
- 4 green cardamom pods
- 4 cloves
- 1 bay leaf
- Fresh coriander leaves for garnish

Instructions:

Heat oil or ghee in a large, heavy-bottomed pan over medium heat.
Add cinnamon stick, green cardamom pods, cloves, and bay leaf. Sauté for a minute until the spices release their aroma.
Add finely chopped onions and sauté until they turn golden brown.
Add ginger-garlic paste and sauté for a minute until the raw smell disappears.
Add chopped tomatoes and cook until they become soft and the oil starts to separate from the mixture.
In a bowl, whisk the yogurt and add ground coriander, ground cumin, turmeric powder, red chili powder, paprika (if using), garam masala, and salt. Mix well.
Add the yogurt-spice mixture to the pan and cook for a few minutes until the oil separates from the masala.
Add the lamb cubes and coat them well with the masala. Cook for 5-7 minutes until the meat is browned.

Add enough water to cover the meat and bring it to a boil. Reduce the heat, cover the pan, and let it simmer until the meat is tender. This may take around 45 minutes to an hour.
Once the meat is cooked, check the consistency of the gravy. Adjust salt and spice levels according to your taste.
Garnish with fresh coriander leaves.

Serve Rogan Josh hot with naan, rice, or Indian bread of your choice. It's a rich and aromatic dish that is sure to delight your taste buds. Enjoy!

Chana Masala

Ingredients:

- 2 cups cooked chickpeas (canned or soaked and boiled)
- 2 tablespoons vegetable oil
- 1 large onion, finely chopped
- 2 tomatoes, chopped
- 1 tablespoon ginger-garlic paste
- 1 green chili, finely chopped (adjust to taste)
- 1 teaspoon cumin seeds
- 1 teaspoon coriander powder
- 1/2 teaspoon turmeric powder
- 1 teaspoon red chili powder (adjust to taste)
- 1 teaspoon garam masala
- 1 teaspoon ground cumin
- Salt to taste
- Fresh coriander leaves for garnish

Instructions:

Heat oil in a pan over medium heat. Add cumin seeds and let them splutter.
Add finely chopped onions and sauté until they become golden brown.
Add ginger-garlic paste and chopped green chili. Sauté for a minute until the raw smell disappears.
Add chopped tomatoes and cook until they become soft and the oil starts to separate from the mixture.
Add coriander powder, turmeric powder, red chili powder, garam masala, ground cumin, and salt. Mix well and cook for a few minutes.
Add the cooked chickpeas to the pan and stir to coat them with the spice mixture.
If the mixture is too dry, you can add a little water at this stage to achieve your desired consistency.
Cover the pan and let it simmer for about 10-15 minutes, allowing the flavors to meld.
Adjust salt and spice levels according to your taste.
Garnish with fresh coriander leaves.

Serve Chana Masala hot with rice, naan, or any Indian bread of your choice. It's a hearty and flavorful dish that's perfect for a satisfying vegetarian meal. Enjoy!

Chicken Korma

Ingredients:

For Marination:

- 500g chicken, cut into pieces
- 1 cup yogurt
- 1 tablespoon ginger-garlic paste
- 1 teaspoon red chili powder
- 1/2 teaspoon turmeric powder
- Salt to taste

For the Korma:

- 1 cup cashews, soaked in warm water for 15-20 minutes
- 2 tablespoons vegetable oil or ghee
- 2 large onions, finely sliced
- 2 tomatoes, chopped
- 1 tablespoon ginger-garlic paste
- 1 teaspoon ground coriander
- 1 teaspoon ground cumin
- 1/2 teaspoon turmeric powder
- 1/2 teaspoon red chili powder (adjust to taste)
- 1/2 teaspoon garam masala
- 1 cup coconut milk (optional)
- Salt to taste
- Fresh coriander leaves for garnish

Instructions:

In a bowl, marinate the chicken with yogurt, ginger-garlic paste, red chili powder, turmeric powder, and salt. Let it marinate for at least 1-2 hours.
In a blender, make a smooth paste by blending soaked cashews with a little water.
Heat oil or ghee in a pan over medium heat. Add sliced onions and sauté until they turn golden brown.
Add ginger-garlic paste and cook for a minute until the raw smell disappears.

Add chopped tomatoes and cook until they become soft and the oil starts to separate from the mixture.
Add ground coriander, ground cumin, turmeric powder, red chili powder, and garam masala. Mix well and cook for a few minutes.
Add the marinated chicken to the pan and cook until it's no longer pink.
Add the cashew paste and mix well.
If using, pour in coconut milk for extra richness and flavor. Adjust the consistency with water if needed.
Season with salt and let the curry simmer on low heat until the chicken is fully cooked and the gravy thickens.
Garnish with fresh coriander leaves.

Serve Chicken Korma hot with naan, rice, or any Indian bread of your choice. It's a comforting and indulgent dish that's sure to please your taste buds. Enjoy!

Dal Makhani

Ingredients:

- 1 cup whole black lentils (urad dal)
- 1/4 cup red kidney beans (rajma)
- 4 cups water (for soaking lentils and beans)
- 2 tablespoons ghee or butter
- 1 large onion, finely chopped
- 2 tomatoes, chopped
- 1 tablespoon ginger-garlic paste
- 1 teaspoon cumin seeds
- 1/2 teaspoon turmeric powder
- 1 teaspoon red chili powder (adjust to taste)
- 1 tablespoon coriander powder
- 1/2 teaspoon garam masala
- Salt to taste
- 1/2 cup cream
- Fresh coriander leaves for garnish

Instructions:

Rinse the whole black lentils and kidney beans under running water. Soak them in water for at least 8 hours or overnight.

Drain the soaked lentils and beans. In a pressure cooker, add the lentils, kidney beans, and 4 cups of water. Pressure cook until they are soft and well-cooked. This may take about 20-25 minutes.

In a pan, heat ghee or butter over medium heat. Add cumin seeds and let them splutter.

Add finely chopped onions and sauté until they turn golden brown.

Add ginger-garlic paste and cook for a minute until the raw smell disappears.

Add chopped tomatoes and cook until they become soft and the oil starts to separate from the mixture.

Add turmeric powder, red chili powder, coriander powder, garam masala, and salt. Mix well and cook for a few minutes.

Add the cooked lentils and kidney beans to the pan. Mix well with the spice mixture.

If the mixture is too thick, add water to achieve your desired consistency. Let it simmer for 15-20 minutes, allowing the flavors to meld.
Stir in cream and cook for an additional 5 minutes.
Garnish with fresh coriander leaves.

Serve Dal Makhani hot with rice, naan, or any Indian bread of your choice. It's a

comforting and indulgent dish that's perfect for a satisfying meal. Enjoy!

Chicken Curry

Ingredients:

- 1 kg chicken, cut into pieces
- 2 large onions, finely chopped
- 2 tomatoes, chopped
- 1 tablespoon ginger-garlic paste
- 2 tablespoons vegetable oil
- 1 teaspoon cumin seeds
- 2 teaspoons coriander powder
- 1 teaspoon turmeric powder
- 1 teaspoon red chili powder (adjust to taste)
- 1 teaspoon garam masala
- Salt to taste
- Fresh coriander leaves for garnish

Instructions:

Heat oil in a large, heavy-bottomed pan over medium heat. Add cumin seeds and let them splutter.
Add finely chopped onions and sauté until they become golden brown.
Add ginger-garlic paste and cook for a minute until the raw smell disappears.
Add chopped tomatoes and cook until they become soft and the oil starts to separate from the mixture.
Add coriander powder, turmeric powder, red chili powder, and salt. Mix well and cook for a few minutes.
Add the chicken pieces to the pan and coat them well with the spice mixture.
Cover the pan and let the chicken cook on low to medium heat, stirring occasionally. The chicken will release its juices, and the curry will thicken as it cooks. This may take about 20-25 minutes.
Once the chicken is cooked, add garam masala and mix well.
Garnish with fresh coriander leaves.

Serve Chicken Curry hot with rice, naan, or any Indian bread of your choice. You can customize this recipe by adding ingredients like yogurt, coconut milk, or various spices based on your taste preferences. Enjoy your homemade Chicken Curry!

Baingan Bharta

Ingredients:

- 1 large eggplant (baingan)
- 2 tablespoons vegetable oil
- 1 teaspoon cumin seeds
- 1 large onion, finely chopped
- 2 tomatoes, chopped
- 1 tablespoon ginger-garlic paste
- 1 green chili, finely chopped (adjust to taste)
- 1 teaspoon ground coriander
- 1/2 teaspoon turmeric powder
- 1 teaspoon red chili powder (adjust to taste)
- 1 teaspoon garam masala
- Salt to taste
- Fresh coriander leaves for garnish

Instructions:

Preheat your oven or grill. Alternatively, you can roast the eggplant directly over a gas flame on the stove.
Prick the eggplant with a fork in a few places. Roast the eggplant until the skin is charred and the inside is soft. This may take about 20-30 minutes in the oven or on the grill, turning occasionally for even roasting.
Allow the roasted eggplant to cool. Once cool, peel off the charred skin and mash the pulp. Discard any large seeds.
In a pan, heat oil over medium heat. Add cumin seeds and let them splutter.
Add finely chopped onions and sauté until they become golden brown.
Add ginger-garlic paste and chopped green chili. Sauté for a minute until the raw smell disappears.
Add chopped tomatoes and cook until they become soft and the oil starts to separate from the mixture.
Add ground coriander, turmeric powder, red chili powder, garam masala, and salt. Mix well and cook for a few minutes.
Add the mashed eggplant to the pan and mix it with the spice mixture. Cook for an additional 5-7 minutes, allowing the flavors to meld.
Garnish with fresh coriander leaves.

Serve Baingan Bharta hot with naan, roti, or any Indian bread of your choice. It's a smoky and flavorful dish that is sure to be enjoyed by eggplant lovers. Enjoy!

Bhindi Masala

Ingredients:

- 500g fresh okra (bhindi), washed and dried
- 2 tablespoons vegetable oil
- 1 teaspoon cumin seeds
- 1 large onion, finely chopped
- 2 tomatoes, chopped
- 1 tablespoon ginger-garlic paste
- 1 green chili, finely chopped (adjust to taste)
- 1 teaspoon ground coriander
- 1/2 teaspoon turmeric powder
- 1 teaspoon red chili powder (adjust to taste)
- 1 teaspoon garam masala
- Salt to taste
- Fresh coriander leaves for garnish

Instructions:

Trim the ends of the okra and cut them into 1-inch pieces.
Heat oil in a pan over medium heat. Add cumin seeds and let them splutter.
Add finely chopped onions and sauté until they become golden brown.
Add ginger-garlic paste and chopped green chili. Sauté for a minute until the raw smell disappears.
Add chopped tomatoes and cook until they become soft and the oil starts to separate from the mixture.
Add ground coriander, turmeric powder, red chili powder, garam masala, and salt. Mix well and cook for a few minutes.
Add the chopped okra to the pan and stir well to coat them with the spice mixture.
Cover the pan and cook on low to medium heat, stirring occasionally. Cook until the okra is tender but still retains its shape. This may take about 15-20 minutes.
Garnish with fresh coriander leaves.

Serve Bhindi Masala hot with roti, naan, or any Indian bread of your choice. It makes for

a delicious and vegetarian side dish that you can enjoy with rice as well. Enjoy!

Dum Aloo

Ingredients:

- 500g baby potatoes, boiled and peeled
- 2 tablespoons vegetable oil
- 1 teaspoon cumin seeds
- 1 large onion, finely chopped
- 2 tomatoes, chopped
- 1 tablespoon ginger-garlic paste
- 1/2 cup yogurt
- 1 teaspoon ground coriander
- 1/2 teaspoon turmeric powder
- 1 teaspoon red chili powder (adjust to taste)
- 1 teaspoon garam masala
- 1 teaspoon ground fennel seeds
- Salt to taste
- Fresh coriander leaves for garnish

For the Dum (slow cooking) process:

- Aluminum foil or dough to seal the lid

Instructions:

Heat oil in a pan over medium heat. Add cumin seeds and let them splutter.
Add finely chopped onions and sauté until they become golden brown.
Add ginger-garlic paste and cook for a minute until the raw smell disappears.
Add chopped tomatoes and cook until they become soft and the oil starts to separate from the mixture.
In a bowl, whisk yogurt and add ground coriander, turmeric powder, red chili powder, garam masala, ground fennel seeds, and salt. Mix well.
Add the yogurt-spice mixture to the pan and cook for a few minutes until the oil separates from the masala.
Add the boiled and peeled baby potatoes to the pan, ensuring they are well-coated with the masala.
Cover the pan with a lid and let the potatoes cook on low heat for about 15-20 minutes, stirring occasionally.

While the potatoes are cooking, prepare the dum (slow cooking) by sealing the lid with aluminum foil or dough to trap the steam. This helps infuse the flavors. Garnish with fresh coriander leaves.

Serve Dum Aloo hot with naan, roti, or any Indian bread of your choice. It's a flavorful and comforting dish that is perfect for a satisfying meal. Enjoy!

Fish Curry

Ingredients:

- 500g fish fillets (any white fish, like tilapia or cod), cleaned and cut into pieces
- 2 tablespoons vegetable oil
- 1 teaspoon mustard seeds
- 1 onion, finely chopped
- 2 tomatoes, chopped
- 1 tablespoon ginger-garlic paste
- 1 teaspoon turmeric powder
- 1 teaspoon red chili powder (adjust to taste)
- 1 teaspoon ground coriander
- 1 teaspoon cumin powder
- 1 cup coconut milk
- Salt to taste
- Fresh coriander leaves for garnish

Instructions:

Heat oil in a pan over medium heat. Add mustard seeds and let them splutter.
Add finely chopped onions and sauté until they become translucent.
Add ginger-garlic paste and cook for a minute until the raw smell disappears.
Add chopped tomatoes and cook until they become soft and the oil starts to separate from the mixture.
Add turmeric powder, red chili powder, ground coriander, and cumin powder. Mix well and cook for a few minutes.
Add coconut milk to the pan and bring it to a gentle simmer.
Add the fish pieces to the simmering curry, ensuring they are well-coated with the sauce.
Cover the pan and let the fish cook in the curry for about 10-15 minutes or until the fish is cooked through.
Adjust salt and spice levels according to your taste.
Garnish with fresh coriander leaves.

Serve the Fish Curry hot with steamed rice or crusty bread. This aromatic and flavorful dish is perfect for seafood lovers. Enjoy!

Keema Samosa

Ingredients:

For the Filling:

- 1 lb ground meat (beef, lamb, or chicken)
- 2 tablespoons oil
- 1 large onion, finely chopped
- 2 teaspoons ginger-garlic paste
- 1 cup peas (fresh or frozen)
- 2 teaspoons ground coriander
- 1 teaspoon ground cumin
- 1/2 teaspoon turmeric powder
- 1/2 teaspoon red chili powder (adjust to taste)
- Salt to taste
- 2 tablespoons chopped cilantro (coriander leaves)
- Juice of half a lemon

For the Samosa Dough:

- 2 cups all-purpose flour
- 1/4 cup ghee (clarified butter) or oil
- 1/2 teaspoon salt
- Water for kneading

Other:

- Oil for deep frying

Instructions:

Prepare the Filling:

In a pan, heat oil and sauté the chopped onions until golden brown.
Add ginger-garlic paste and cook for a minute until the raw smell disappears.
Add the ground meat and cook until it's browned.
Add peas, ground coriander, ground cumin, turmeric powder, red chili powder, and salt.
Mix well and cook until the meat is fully cooked.
Stir in chopped cilantro and lemon juice. Remove from heat and let the filling cool.

Make the Samosa Dough:

In a mixing bowl, combine the all-purpose flour, ghee (or oil), and salt.
Gradually add water and knead to form a smooth and firm dough. Cover the dough and
let it rest for about 30 minutes.

Shape and Fill the Samosas:

Divide the dough into small balls and roll each ball into a thin oval or round shape.
Cut the rolled dough in half to form two semi-circles.
Fold each semi-circle into a cone, sealing the edges with a little water to form a
triangular pocket.
Fill each pocket with the keema filling, ensuring it's not overfilled.
Seal the open edge of the triangular pocket, pinching the edges together to form a
sealed samosa.

Deep Fry the Samosas:

Heat oil in a deep frying pan over medium heat.
Once the oil is hot, carefully slide in the samosas, a few at a time, and fry until they are
golden brown and crispy.
Remove the samosas from the oil and place them on paper towels to absorb excess oil.

Serve:

Allow the Keema Samosas to cool slightly before serving.
Serve them with mint chutney, tamarind chutney, or your favorite dipping sauce.
Enjoy the flavorful and crispy Keema Samosas!

These homemade Keema Samosas are a delightful treat, perfect for snacking or as a starter for
gatherings. The combination of spiced meat encased in a crispy pastry shell makes them a
popular and satisfying snack.

Vegetable Biryani

Ingredients:

For the Rice:

- 1 cup basmati rice
- 2 cups water
- 1 bay leaf
- 2-3 green cardamom pods
- 2-3 cloves
- Salt to taste

For the Vegetable Mix:

- 1 cup mixed vegetables (carrots, peas, beans, potatoes), chopped
- 1 large onion, thinly sliced
- 1 tomato, chopped
- 1/2 cup plain yogurt
- 2 tablespoons biryani masala
- 1 teaspoon red chili powder
- 1/2 teaspoon turmeric powder
- Salt to taste
- 2 tablespoons oil

For Layering:

- Fresh coriander leaves, chopped
- Fresh mint leaves, chopped
- Fried onions (optional)
- Ghee (clarified butter)

Instructions:

1. Cook the Basmati Rice:

    Rinse the basmati rice under cold water until the water runs clear.
    In a pot, bring 2 cups of water to a boil. Add the rinsed rice, bay leaf, green cardamom pods, cloves, and salt.
    Cook the rice until it's 70-80% done. It should still have a slight bite to it. Drain the rice and set it aside.

2. Prepare the Vegetable Mix:

In a pan, heat oil and sauté the sliced onions until golden brown.
Add the chopped tomatoes and cook until they are soft.
Add the mixed vegetables, biryani masala, red chili powder, turmeric powder, and salt.
Cook until the vegetables are slightly tender.
Stir in the plain yogurt and cook for a few more minutes until the mixture is well combined.

3. Layering:

Preheat your oven to 350°F (180°C).
In an oven-safe dish, layer half of the partially cooked basmati rice.
Add the cooked vegetable mixture on top of the rice, spreading it evenly.
Sprinkle chopped coriander leaves and mint leaves over the vegetables. Optionally, add a layer of fried onions for added flavor.
Cover the vegetable layer with the remaining partially cooked basmati rice.
Drizzle ghee over the top layer of rice.

4. Dum Cooking (Oven or Stovetop):

Oven Method:

Cover the dish with a tight-fitting lid or aluminum foil.
Bake in the preheated oven for 20-25 minutes or until the rice is fully cooked and aromatic.

Stovetop Method:

Place the covered dish on a tawa (griddle) or a flat pan.
Cook on low heat for 20-25 minutes, allowing the biryani to cook in its steam.

5. Serve:

Gently fluff the Vegetable Biryani with a fork, mixing the layers.
Garnish with additional chopped coriander and mint leaves.
Serve hot with raita, yogurt, or a side salad.

Enjoy the fragrant and flavorful Vegetable Biryani, a classic Indian dish that's perfect for special occasions or a hearty meal!

Chicken Saag

Ingredients:

For Marinating Chicken:

- 1 lb (450g) boneless, skinless chicken pieces, cut into bite-sized cubes
- 1/2 cup yogurt
- 1 teaspoon ginger-garlic paste
- 1 teaspoon red chili powder
- 1/2 teaspoon turmeric powder
- Salt to taste

For the Saag Sauce:

- 4 cups fresh spinach leaves, washed and chopped
- 1 cup fenugreek leaves (methi), washed and chopped (optional)
- 1 large onion, finely chopped
- 2 tomatoes, chopped
- 2 green chilies, chopped
- 1 tablespoon ginger-garlic paste
- 1 teaspoon cumin seeds
- 1 teaspoon coriander powder
- 1 teaspoon cumin powder
- 1/2 teaspoon turmeric powder
- 1/2 teaspoon garam masala
- 1/2 cup cream (optional)
- 2 tablespoons oil or ghee
- Salt to taste

For Tempering:

- 1 tablespoon ghee
- 1 teaspoon cumin seeds
- 2-3 garlic cloves, minced
- 1/2 teaspoon red chili powder

Instructions:

1. Marinate the Chicken:

   In a bowl, mix yogurt, ginger-garlic paste, red chili powder, turmeric powder, and salt.

Add chicken pieces to the marinade, ensuring they are well-coated. Marinate for at least 30 minutes.

2. Cook the Chicken:

Heat oil or ghee in a pan. Add cumin seeds and let them splutter.
Add finely chopped onions and sauté until golden brown.
Add ginger-garlic paste and green chilies. Sauté for a minute until the raw smell disappears.
Add chopped tomatoes and cook until they become soft and the oil starts to separate.
Add coriander powder, cumin powder, turmeric powder, and garam masala. Mix well.
Add marinated chicken pieces and cook until they are browned and cooked through.

3. Prepare the Saag Sauce:

In a separate pot, blanch chopped spinach and fenugreek leaves in hot water for 2-3 minutes. Drain and transfer them to a blender. Blend into a smooth puree.
Add the spinach puree to the cooked chicken and mix well.
Cook for 5-7 minutes, allowing the flavors to meld.
If using cream, add it now and stir until well combined. Adjust salt and spices according to your taste.

4. Prepare the Tempering:

In a small pan, heat ghee. Add cumin seeds and let them splutter.
Add minced garlic and sauté until it turns golden brown.
Add red chili powder and immediately pour this tempering over the Chicken Saag. Mix gently.

5. Serve:

Chicken Saag is ready to be served. Garnish with a drizzle of cream and chopped coriander if desired.
Serve hot with naan, rice, or your favorite Indian bread.

Enjoy the wholesome and flavorful Chicken Saag, a comforting dish that combines the richness of chicken with the goodness of spinach and aromatic spices!

Masoor Dal

Ingredients:

- 1 cup masoor dal (red lentils), washed and soaked for 30 minutes
- 1 large onion, finely chopped
- 1 large tomato, chopped
- 1 green chili, chopped
- 1 teaspoon ginger-garlic paste
- 1/2 teaspoon turmeric powder
- 1 teaspoon red chili powder (adjust to taste)
- 1 teaspoon cumin powder
- 1 teaspoon coriander powder
- Salt to taste
- 1 tablespoon ghee or oil
- 1 teaspoon cumin seeds
- A pinch of asafoetida (hing)
- Fresh coriander leaves for garnish
- Lemon wedges for serving

Instructions:

1. Cook the Lentils:

   In a pressure cooker or a pot, add soaked and washed masoor dal along with 3 cups of water.
   Add turmeric powder, red chili powder, cumin powder, coriander powder, chopped tomato, green chili, and ginger-garlic paste.
   Pressure cook for about 3-4 whistles or simmer in a pot until the lentils are soft and cooked through.
   Once cooked, whisk the dal to make it smooth and creamy. Add salt to taste.

2. Prepare the Tempering:

   In a separate pan, heat ghee or oil.
   Add cumin seeds and let them splutter.
   Add chopped onions and sauté until they become golden brown.
   Add a pinch of asafoetida (hing) for flavor.

3. Combine Dal and Tempering:

   Pour the tempering over the cooked lentils and mix well.

Simmer the dal for a few more minutes, allowing the flavors to meld.

4. Garnish and Serve:

Garnish the Masoor Dal with fresh coriander leaves.
Squeeze some lemon juice on top before serving for a burst of freshness.
Serve hot with steamed rice or your favorite Indian bread (roti, naan).

Masoor Dal is not only delicious but also packed with protein and essential nutrients. Enjoy this comforting and wholesome lentil curry as a part of your everyday meals.

Chicken Tikka Masala

Ingredients:

For Chicken Marinade:

- 1 lb (450g) boneless, skinless chicken thighs or breasts, cut into bite-sized pieces
- 1 cup yogurt
- 1 tablespoon ginger-garlic paste
- 1 tablespoon red chili powder
- 1 teaspoon turmeric powder
- 1 teaspoon garam masala
- Salt to taste
- 2 tablespoons vegetable oil

For Chicken Tikka:

- Vegetable oil for grilling or broiling
- Skewers for grilling (wooden skewers soaked in water for 30 minutes)

For Masala Sauce:

- 2 tablespoons vegetable oil
- 1 large onion, finely chopped
- 2 tomatoes, pureed
- 1 tablespoon tomato paste
- 1 tablespoon ginger-garlic paste
- 1 teaspoon ground cumin
- 1 teaspoon ground coriander
- 1 teaspoon red chili powder (adjust to taste)
- 1 teaspoon turmeric powder
- 1 teaspoon garam masala
- 1 cup heavy cream or coconut milk
- Salt to taste
- Fresh coriander leaves for garnish

Instructions:

1. Marinate the Chicken:

    In a bowl, mix yogurt, ginger-garlic paste, red chili powder, turmeric powder, garam masala, salt, and vegetable oil to create the marinade.

Add chicken pieces to the marinade, ensuring they are well-coated. Marinate for at least 2 hours, or preferably overnight in the refrigerator.

2. Chicken Tikka:

Preheat your grill or broiler.
Thread marinated chicken pieces onto skewers.
Grill or broil the chicken until fully cooked and slightly charred on the edges. Rotate the skewers for even cooking.

3. Prepare the Masala Sauce:

In a pan, heat vegetable oil. Add chopped onions and sauté until golden brown.
Add ginger-garlic paste and cook for a minute until the raw smell disappears.
Add ground cumin, ground coriander, red chili powder, turmeric powder, and garam masala. Sauté for 1-2 minutes.
Add pureed tomatoes and tomato paste. Cook until the oil starts to separate from the masala.
Pour in heavy cream or coconut milk, stirring continuously. Add salt to taste.
Simmer the sauce for 5-7 minutes until it thickens.

4. Combine Chicken Tikka and Masala Sauce:

Add the grilled chicken tikka pieces to the masala sauce. Mix well.
Allow the chicken to simmer in the sauce for an additional 10-15 minutes, ensuring it absorbs the flavors.

5. Garnish and Serve:

Garnish with fresh coriander leaves.
Serve hot with naan, rice, or your favorite Indian bread.

Enjoy the rich and creamy Chicken Tikka Masala, a classic Indian dish that's sure to delight your taste buds!

Pani Puri

Ingredients:

For Pani (Spiced Water):

- 1 cup mint leaves
- 1/2 cup coriander leaves
- 2 green chilies
- 1-inch piece of ginger
- 1 tablespoon tamarind pulp
- 1 teaspoon roasted cumin powder
- 1 teaspoon chaat masala
- 1/2 teaspoon black salt
- Salt to taste
- 4 cups cold water

For Puri:

- Pani Puri puris (available at Indian grocery stores)
- Boiled and mashed potatoes
- Boiled chickpeas
- Tamarind chutney
- Chopped onions (optional)
- Sev (crispy chickpea noodles, optional)

Instructions:

1. Prepare Pani (Spiced Water):

In a blender, combine mint leaves, coriander leaves, green chilies, and ginger. Blend into a smooth paste.
Strain the paste to extract the juice. You can use a fine mesh sieve or cheesecloth.
In a large bowl, mix the extracted juice with tamarind pulp, roasted cumin powder, chaat masala, black salt, and regular salt.
Add cold water and mix well to create the spiced water (pani). Adjust the seasoning according to your taste.

2. Assemble Pani Puri:

Gently make a small hole in the center of each puri using your thumb or a spoon.
Fill each puri with a spoonful of mashed potatoes and boiled chickpeas.

Drizzle a little tamarind chutney inside each puri.
Place the filled puris on a serving plate.

3. Serve:

Just before serving, pour the prepared spiced water (pani) into each puri using a spoon
or a small ladle.
Optionally, you can add chopped onions and sev on top for extra crunch.
Serve immediately and enjoy the burst of flavors in each Pani Puri!

Pani Puri is best enjoyed fresh, and it's a fun and interactive way to experience the diverse tastes
of Indian street food.

Rajma

Ingredients:

- 1 cup dried red kidney beans (rajma), soaked overnight
- 2 tablespoons oil or ghee
- 1 large onion, finely chopped
- 2 tomatoes, pureed
- 1 tablespoon ginger-garlic paste
- 1-2 green chilies, chopped (adjust to taste)
- 1 teaspoon cumin seeds
- 1 teaspoon coriander powder
- 1/2 teaspoon turmeric powder
- 1 teaspoon red chili powder (adjust to taste)
- 1 teaspoon garam masala
- Salt to taste
- Fresh coriander leaves for garnish

Instructions:

1. Cook the Rajma:

   Rinse the soaked kidney beans and pressure cook them with enough water and a pinch
   of salt until they are soft and well-cooked. This may take about 3-4 whistles or around
   20-25 minutes.
   Once cooked, set aside.

2. Prepare the Gravy:

   Heat oil or ghee in a pan. Add cumin seeds and let them splutter.
   Add chopped onions and sauté until golden brown.
   Add ginger-garlic paste and chopped green chilies. Sauté for a minute until the raw smell
   disappears.
   Add pureed tomatoes and cook until the oil starts to separate from the masala.
   Add coriander powder, turmeric powder, red chili powder, and salt. Mix well and cook for
   a couple of minutes.

3. Combine Rajma and Gravy:

   Add the cooked kidney beans (rajma) to the tomato gravy. Mix well.
   Add garam masala and adjust the consistency by adding water if needed. Simmer for
   10-15 minutes, allowing the flavors to meld.

4. Garnish and Serve:

    Garnish with fresh coriander leaves.
    Serve hot with steamed rice or Indian bread like roti or naan.

Rajma is a hearty and comforting dish, rich in protein and flavors. Enjoy this delicious North Indian classic as a main course in your meals.

Malai Kofta

Ingredients:

For Koftas (Dumplings):

- 2 cups grated paneer (Indian cottage cheese)
- 1 cup boiled and mashed potatoes
- 2 tablespoons cornflour or besan (gram flour)
- Salt to taste
- 1 teaspoon red chili powder
- 1 teaspoon garam masala
- Oil for deep frying

For Gravy:

- 2 tablespoons oil or ghee
- 1 large onion, finely chopped
- 2 tomatoes, pureed
- 1 tablespoon ginger-garlic paste
- 1 teaspoon cumin seeds
- 1 teaspoon coriander powder
- 1/2 teaspoon turmeric powder
- 1 teaspoon red chili powder
- 1 teaspoon garam masala
- 1/2 cup cashew nuts, soaked in warm water
- 1/2 cup fresh cream
- Salt to taste
- Fresh coriander leaves for garnish

Instructions:

For Koftas (Dumplings):

In a bowl, combine grated paneer, mashed potatoes, cornflour or besan, salt, red chili powder, and garam masala.
Mix well to form a smooth and firm dough.
Divide the mixture into small portions and shape them into round or oval koftas.
Heat oil for deep frying. Fry the koftas until golden brown and crispy. Remove and set aside on paper towels to drain excess oil.

For Gravy:

In a blender, make a smooth paste of soaked cashew nuts by adding a little water.
Heat oil or ghee in a pan. Add cumin seeds and let them splutter.
Add finely chopped onions and sauté until golden brown.
Add ginger-garlic paste and sauté for a minute until the raw smell disappears.
Add coriander powder, turmeric powder, red chili powder, and garam masala. Cook for
1-2 minutes.
Add pureed tomatoes and cook until the oil starts to separate from the masala.
Add the cashew nut paste and mix well.
Pour in fresh cream, stir, and simmer the gravy for a few minutes.
Add salt to taste and adjust the consistency by adding water if needed.

Assemble Malai Kofta:

Just before serving, place the fried koftas in the serving dish.
Pour the hot creamy gravy over the koftas.
Garnish with fresh coriander leaves.
Serve Malai Kofta hot with naan, roti, or steamed rice.

Malai Kofta is a rich and indulgent dish, perfect for special occasions or when you want to treat

yourself to a delicious homemade curry.

Chicken Vindaloo

Ingredients:

For Marination:

- 1 kg (2.2 lbs) chicken, cut into curry pieces
- 1 teaspoon turmeric powder
- 1 teaspoon red chili powder
- 1 teaspoon cumin powder
- 1 teaspoon coriander powder
- Salt to taste
- 1 cup plain yogurt

For Vindaloo Paste:

- 2 tablespoons white vinegar
- 8-10 dried red chilies, soaked in warm water
- 1 tablespoon cumin seeds
- 1 tablespoon black mustard seeds
- 1 tablespoon fenugreek seeds
- 1 tablespoon peppercorns
- 1 teaspoon turmeric powder
- 8-10 garlic cloves
- 1-inch ginger, chopped

For the Curry:

- 3 tablespoons oil
- 2 large onions, finely sliced
- 3 tomatoes, chopped
- Salt to taste
- 1 cup water (adjust as needed)
- Fresh cilantro for garnish

Instructions:

Start by marinating the chicken. In a bowl, mix the chicken with turmeric powder, red chili powder, cumin powder, coriander powder, salt, and yogurt. Allow it to marinate for at least 1-2 hours or overnight in the refrigerator.

Prepare the vindaloo paste by blending all the paste ingredients in a food processor or blender until you get a smooth consistency.
Heat oil in a large pot or deep skillet over medium heat. Add the sliced onions and sauté until golden brown.
Add the vindaloo paste to the pot and cook for a few minutes until the oil starts to separate from the paste.
Add the marinated chicken to the pot and cook for 5-7 minutes, stirring occasionally.
Add chopped tomatoes and salt. Cook until the tomatoes are soft and the oil separates from the masala.
Pour in water and bring the curry to a boil. Reduce the heat, cover the pot, and let it simmer until the chicken is cooked through and the curry has thickened.
Garnish with fresh cilantro and serve the Chicken Vindaloo hot with steamed rice or Indian bread (naan or roti).

Adjust the spice levels and consistency according to your preference. Enjoy your homemade Chicken Vindaloo!

Methi Thepla

Ingredients:

- 2 cups whole wheat flour
- 1 cup fresh fenugreek leaves (methi), washed and chopped
- 2 tablespoons yogurt
- 1 tablespoon besan (gram flour)
- 1 teaspoon turmeric powder
- 1 teaspoon red chili powder
- 1 teaspoon coriander powder
- 1/2 teaspoon cumin powder
- 1/2 teaspoon ajwain (carom seeds)
- 1/2 teaspoon sesame seeds
- Salt to taste
- 1 tablespoon oil
- Water, as needed, for kneading the dough
- Ghee or oil for cooking

Instructions:

In a large mixing bowl, combine whole wheat flour, chopped fenugreek leaves, yogurt, besan, turmeric powder, red chili powder, coriander powder, cumin powder, ajwain, sesame seeds, salt, and 1 tablespoon of oil.

Mix the ingredients well, and then gradually add water to knead a smooth and soft dough. The fenugreek leaves will release some water, so adjust the consistency accordingly.

Cover the dough and let it rest for about 15-20 minutes.

Divide the dough into small lemon-sized balls.

Heat a tawa (griddle) or a non-stick pan over medium heat.

Take a portion of the dough, flatten it with your hands, and then roll it into a thin, round disc using a rolling pin. Dust the surface with some dry flour to prevent sticking.

Place the rolled Methi Thepla on the hot griddle. Cook for a minute or until small bubbles appear on the surface.

Flip it over and apply ghee or oil on the cooked side. Flip again and apply ghee or oil on the other side.

Cook until both sides are golden brown and have crispy edges.

Repeat the process with the remaining dough balls.

Serve Methi Thepla warm with yogurt, pickle, or any chutney of your choice. It makes for a delicious and wholesome meal, perfect for breakfast or as a snack.

Egg Curry

Ingredients:

- 6 hard-boiled eggs, peeled and halved
- 2 large onions, finely chopped
- 2 tomatoes, pureed
- 2 green chilies, chopped
- 1 tablespoon ginger-garlic paste
- 1/2 cup plain yogurt
- 1 teaspoon cumin seeds
- 1 teaspoon mustard seeds
- 1 teaspoon turmeric powder
- 1 teaspoon red chili powder (adjust to taste)
- 1 teaspoon coriander powder
- 1/2 teaspoon garam masala
- Salt to taste
- 2 tablespoons oil
- Fresh coriander leaves for garnish

Instructions:

Heat oil in a pan over medium heat. Add cumin seeds and mustard seeds. Allow them to splutter.
Add chopped onions and cook until they become golden brown.
Add ginger-garlic paste and chopped green chilies. Sauté for a couple of minutes until the raw aroma disappears.
Add tomato puree and cook until the oil separates from the masala.
Reduce the heat and add turmeric powder, red chili powder, coriander powder, and salt. Mix well and cook for a few minutes.
Whisk the yogurt in a bowl and gradually add it to the masala, stirring continuously to prevent curdling.
Once the masala is well-cooked and the oil floats on top, add garam masala and mix.
Gently add the halved boiled eggs to the curry, ensuring they are well-coated with the masala.
Add water to achieve the desired consistency for the curry. Bring it to a simmer, cover the pan, and let it cook for 10-15 minutes on low heat.
Garnish with fresh coriander leaves before serving.

Serve the Egg Curry with steamed rice, naan, or crusty bread. Adjust the spice levels according to your taste preference, and feel free to customize the recipe with additional spices or ingredients if desired.

Aloo Paratha

Ingredients:

For the Dough:

- 2 cups whole wheat flour
- Water, as needed
- Salt, a pinch

For the Potato Filling:

- 3 to 4 medium-sized potatoes, boiled, peeled, and mashed
- 1 small onion, finely chopped
- 1 or 2 green chilies, finely chopped
- 1 teaspoon ginger, grated
- 1 teaspoon cumin seeds
- 1/2 teaspoon red chili powder
- 1/2 teaspoon garam masala
- 1/2 teaspoon amchur (dry mango powder)
- Salt, to taste
- Fresh coriander leaves, chopped
- Ghee or oil, for cooking

Instructions:

For the Dough:

In a large mixing bowl, combine whole wheat flour, a pinch of salt, and water gradually to form a soft and smooth dough.
Knead the dough for a few minutes, cover it with a damp cloth, and let it rest for about 15-20 minutes.

For the Potato Filling:

In a mixing bowl, combine the mashed potatoes with chopped onions, green chilies, ginger, cumin seeds, red chili powder, garam masala, amchur, salt, and fresh coriander leaves.
Mix the ingredients well to form a uniform potato filling.

Assembling and Cooking Aloo Paratha:

Divide the dough into equal-sized portions and roll each portion into a ball.
Roll out one dough ball into a small circle on a floured surface.
Place a portion of the potato filling in the center of the rolled-out dough.
Bring the edges of the dough together to cover the filling and seal it, shaping it into a round ball.
Flatten the stuffed ball gently and roll it out into a paratha, ensuring the filling is evenly distributed.
Heat a tawa (griddle) or a non-stick pan over medium heat.
Place the rolled Aloo Paratha on the hot griddle. Cook for a minute, then flip it over.
Spread ghee or oil on the cooked side, then flip again and cook until both sides are golden brown and have crisp spots.
Repeat the process with the remaining dough balls.

Serve the Aloo Paratha hot with yogurt, pickles, or raita. Enjoy this delicious and comforting Indian flatbread!

Tandoori Roti

Ingredients:

- 2 cups whole wheat flour
- Water, as needed
- Salt, a pinch
- 1 tablespoon yogurt (optional)
- 1 tablespoon oil or ghee (optional)

Instructions:

In a large mixing bowl, combine whole wheat flour, a pinch of salt, and yogurt (if using).

Gradually add water and knead the flour to form a soft and smooth dough. Add a little oil or ghee to the dough and continue kneading for a few more minutes.

Cover the dough with a damp cloth and let it rest for at least 30 minutes. This helps the gluten relax and makes the rotis softer.

Divide the dough into equal-sized portions and roll each portion into a ball.

Preheat a tawa (griddle) or a non-stick pan on medium-high heat.

Take one dough ball, dip it in dry flour, and roll it out into a thin, round roti on a floured surface. Ensure that the roti is not too thick.

Carefully place the rolled roti on the hot tawa. Cook for about 30 seconds to 1 minute or until bubbles start to appear on the surface.

Flip the roti and cook the other side for another 30 seconds to 1 minute. You can press the edges lightly with a kitchen towel to help it puff up.

If you have a gas stove, you can directly place the roti on the open flame using tongs for a few seconds to puff it up. Be cautious and rotate it quickly to avoid burning.

Remove the cooked Tandoori Roti from the tawa and apply ghee or butter if desired.

Repeat the process with the remaining dough portions.

Serve Tandoori Roti hot with your favorite curry, dal, or yogurt. It's a versatile and delicious accompaniment to various Indian dishes.

Chicken Bharta

Ingredients:

For Chicken Marinade:

- 500 grams boneless chicken, cooked and shredded
- 1 cup yogurt
- 1 tablespoon ginger-garlic paste
- 1 teaspoon turmeric powder
- 1 teaspoon red chili powder
- Salt to taste

For Gravy:

- 2 tablespoons oil or ghee
- 1 large onion, finely chopped
- 2 tomatoes, pureed
- 1 tablespoon tomato paste (optional)
- 1 tablespoon ginger-garlic paste
- 1 teaspoon cumin powder
- 1 teaspoon coriander powder
- 1/2 teaspoon garam masala
- 1/2 teaspoon turmeric powder
- 1/2 teaspoon red chili powder (adjust to taste)
- Salt to taste
- Fresh coriander leaves for garnish
- Cream or butter for finishing (optional)

Instructions:

Chicken Marinade:

In a bowl, combine shredded chicken, yogurt, ginger-garlic paste, turmeric powder, red chili powder, and salt. Mix well and let it marinate for at least 30 minutes.

Cooking Chicken:

Heat oil or ghee in a pan over medium heat.

Add chopped onions and sauté until golden brown.
Add ginger-garlic paste and cook for a minute until the raw aroma disappears.
Add the pureed tomatoes and tomato paste (if using). Cook until the oil separates from the masala.
Add cumin powder, coriander powder, garam masala, turmeric powder, red chili powder, and salt. Mix well.

Adding Marinated Chicken:

Add the marinated chicken to the pan and mix it well with the masala.
Cook for 10-15 minutes on low heat, allowing the chicken to absorb the flavors of the spices.
Stir occasionally to prevent sticking to the bottom of the pan.

Finishing Touch:

Garnish with fresh coriander leaves.
Optionally, add a dollop of cream or a bit of butter for a rich and creamy texture.

Serve Chicken Bharta hot with naan, roti, or rice. It's a delicious and comforting dish with a perfect blend of spices and flavors. Adjust the spice levels according to your preference.

Vegetable Pakora

Ingredients:

For the Pakora Batter:

- 1 cup chickpea flour (besan)
- 2 tablespoons rice flour
- 1 teaspoon cumin powder
- 1 teaspoon coriander powder
- 1/2 teaspoon turmeric powder
- 1/2 teaspoon red chili powder (adjust to taste)
- Salt to taste
- Water (as needed to make a thick batter)

For the Vegetable Mix:

- 1 cup mixed vegetables (such as onions, potatoes, spinach, cauliflower, and bell peppers), finely chopped or thinly sliced
- 1/4 cup chopped cilantro (coriander leaves)

Other Ingredients:

- Oil for deep frying

Instructions:

In a mixing bowl, combine chickpea flour, rice flour, cumin powder, coriander powder, turmeric powder, red chili powder, and salt.
Gradually add water to the dry ingredients and whisk to form a thick, smooth batter without lumps. The consistency should be thick enough to coat the vegetables.
Add the chopped vegetables and cilantro to the batter. Mix well, ensuring that all the vegetables are coated evenly with the batter.
Heat oil in a deep frying pan over medium heat.

Once the oil is hot, drop spoonfuls of the vegetable batter into the oil. Fry the pakoras until they turn golden brown and crisp. Make sure to flip them for even cooking.
Using a slotted spoon, remove the pakoras from the oil and place them on a plate lined with paper towels to absorb excess oil.
Serve the vegetable pakoras hot with your favorite chutney or sauce.

Enjoy your homemade Vegetable Pakoras! They make for a delightful snack or appetizer

for any occasion.

Aloo Matar

Ingredients:

- 2 cups potatoes, peeled and diced
- 1 cup green peas (fresh or frozen)
- 1 large onion, finely chopped
- 2 tomatoes, finely chopped
- 2 cloves garlic, minced
- 1-inch ginger, grated
- 1 or 2 green chilies, finely chopped (adjust to taste)
- 1 teaspoon cumin seeds
- 1 teaspoon turmeric powder
- 1 teaspoon red chili powder (adjust to taste)
- 1 teaspoon coriander powder
- 1/2 teaspoon garam masala
- Salt to taste
- 2 tablespoons cooking oil
- Fresh cilantro (coriander leaves) for garnish

Instructions:

Heat oil in a pan over medium heat. Add cumin seeds and let them splutter.
Add finely chopped onions and sauté until they become translucent.
Add minced garlic, grated ginger, and chopped green chilies. Sauté for another minute until the raw smell disappears.
Add finely chopped tomatoes and cook until they become soft and the oil starts to separate.
Add turmeric powder, red chili powder, coriander powder, and salt. Mix well and cook for a couple of minutes.
Add diced potatoes and green peas. Mix the vegetables with the spice mixture.
Add water to the pan, cover, and let it simmer until the potatoes and peas are tender. Stir occasionally to prevent sticking.
Once the vegetables are cooked, add garam masala and mix well. Adjust salt and spices according to your taste.
Garnish with fresh cilantro (coriander leaves).
Serve hot with roti, naan, or rice.

Enjoy your Aloo Matar! It's a comforting and flavorful dish that can be enjoyed as a main course with Indian bread or rice.

Hyderabadi Biryani

Ingredients:

For the Marinade:

- 500g chicken, cut into pieces
- 1 cup yogurt
- 1 tablespoon ginger-garlic paste
- 1 teaspoon red chili powder
- 1/2 teaspoon turmeric powder
- 1 teaspoon biryani masala
- Salt to taste
- Fresh coriander and mint leaves, chopped

For the Rice:

- 2 cups basmati rice, soaked for 30 minutes
- 4-5 cups water for cooking rice
- 2-3 green cardamom pods
- 2-3 cloves
- 1 bay leaf
- Salt to taste

For the Biryani:

- 3 large onions, thinly sliced
- 1/2 cup cooking oil or ghee
- 2 tablespoons biryani masala
- Saffron strands soaked in warm milk (optional)
- Ghee for drizzling (optional)

Instructions:

Marinating the Chicken:
- In a bowl, combine the chicken with yogurt, ginger-garlic paste, red chili powder, turmeric powder, biryani masala, salt, and chopped coriander-mint leaves. Marinate for at least 2 hours or overnight for the best flavor.

Cooking the Rice:
- Boil water in a large pot and add soaked basmati rice.

- Add green cardamom pods, cloves, bay leaf, and salt to the boiling water.
- Cook the rice until it is 70-80% done. Drain the water and set aside.

Frying Onions:

- In a separate pan, heat oil or ghee and fry thinly sliced onions until golden brown. Set aside some fried onions for garnishing.

Layering and Dum Cooking:

- In a heavy-bottomed pot or handi, layer half of the partially cooked rice.
- Add the marinated chicken over the rice and spread it evenly.
- Sprinkle biryani masala and half of the fried onions on top of the chicken.
- Add the remaining partially cooked rice as the next layer.
- Drizzle saffron-infused milk on top and garnish with the remaining fried onions.
- Optionally, drizzle some ghee on top for added richness.

Dum Cooking:

- Seal the pot with a tight-fitting lid or aluminum foil. Cook on low heat for 20-25 minutes. This method is known as dum cooking, allowing the flavors to infuse and the rice and chicken to cook together.

Serve:

- Gently fluff the rice with a fork, ensuring not to break the grains.
- Serve the Hyderabadi Biryani hot, garnished with fresh coriander and mint leaves.

Enjoy your flavorful and aromatic Hyderabadi Dum Biryani!

Murg Malaiwala

Ingredients:

For the Marinade:

- 500g boneless chicken, cut into bite-sized pieces
- 1 cup thick yogurt
- 1/2 cup fresh cream (malai)
- 2 tablespoons grated paneer (optional)
- 1 tablespoon ginger-garlic paste
- 1 teaspoon garam masala
- 1 teaspoon ground white pepper
- 1/2 teaspoon turmeric powder
- 1 teaspoon coriander powder
- 1 teaspoon cumin powder
- Salt to taste
- Juice of 1 lemon

For Grilling/Baking:

- Skewers (if grilling)
- Cooking oil or ghee for brushing

For Garnish:

- Chopped coriander leaves
- Lemon wedges
- Onion rings

Instructions:

Marinating the Chicken:
- In a bowl, combine yogurt, fresh cream, grated paneer (if using), ginger-garlic paste, garam masala, white pepper, turmeric powder, coriander powder, cumin powder, salt, and lemon juice. Mix well to form a smooth marinade.

Marination of Chicken:

- Add the chicken pieces to the marinade, ensuring each piece is well-coated. Cover the bowl and refrigerate for at least 2-4 hours, or preferably overnight for the flavors to develop.

Grilling/Baking:

- If grilling, preheat your grill. If baking, preheat your oven to 180°C (356°F).
- Thread the marinated chicken pieces onto skewers if grilling.
- Grill or bake the chicken until it is cooked through and has a nice golden brown color. This usually takes about 15-20 minutes.

Basting (Optional):

- If grilling, you can baste the chicken with a little oil or ghee during the cooking process to keep it moist.

Serve:

- Once cooked, transfer the Murg Malaiwala to a serving platter.
- Garnish with chopped coriander leaves and serve with lemon wedges and onion rings on the side.

Murg Malaiwala can be served as an appetizer or as part of a main course with naan or rice. Enjoy the creamy and flavorful goodness of this delicious dish!

Lauki Kofta

Ingredients:

For Koftas:

- 2 cups grated bottle gourd (lauki)
- 1/2 cup besan (gram flour)
- 1/2 teaspoon cumin powder
- 1/2 teaspoon coriander powder
- 1/4 teaspoon turmeric powder
- 1/2 teaspoon red chili powder (adjust to taste)
- Salt to taste
- Oil for frying

For Curry:

- 2 cups tomato puree
- 1 large onion, finely chopped
- 2 teaspoons ginger-garlic paste
- 1/2 teaspoon cumin seeds
- 1/2 teaspoon turmeric powder
- 1 teaspoon red chili powder (adjust to taste)
- 1 teaspoon coriander powder
- 1/2 teaspoon garam masala
- 1/2 cup cream or cashew paste (optional for richness)
- Salt to taste
- Fresh coriander leaves for garnish

Instructions:

For Koftas:

Squeeze out excess water from the grated bottle gourd.
In a bowl, combine grated bottle gourd, besan, cumin powder, coriander powder,
turmeric powder, red chili powder, and salt. Mix well to form a dough.
Heat oil in a pan for frying.

Take small portions of the mixture and shape them into round or oval dumplings.
Fry the koftas until they are golden brown and crispy. Remove and place them on
a paper towel to absorb excess oil.

For Curry:

In a pan, heat oil. Add cumin seeds and let them splutter.
Add finely chopped onions and sauté until they turn golden brown.
Add ginger-garlic paste and sauté for a minute until the raw smell disappears.
Add turmeric powder, red chili powder, coriander powder, and salt. Cook the
masala until the oil starts to separate.
Add tomato puree and cook until the mixture thickens and the oil separates.
Add garam masala and cream or cashew paste if using. Mix well.
Add water to achieve the desired consistency for the curry. Adjust salt and spices
according to your taste.
Just before serving, add the fried koftas to the curry. Let it simmer for a few
minutes to allow the koftas to absorb the flavors of the curry.
Garnish with fresh coriander leaves.

Serve Lauki Kofta with steamed rice, naan, or roti. Enjoy your delicious and nutritious

bottle gourd kofta curry!

Chicken 65

Ingredients:

For Marination:

- 500g boneless chicken, cut into bite-sized pieces
- 1 cup yogurt
- 1 tablespoon ginger-garlic paste
- 1 teaspoon red chili powder (adjust to taste)
- 1/2 teaspoon turmeric powder
- 1 teaspoon garam masala
- 1 tablespoon cornflour
- 1 tablespoon all-purpose flour (maida)
- Salt to taste
- 1 tablespoon lemon juice

For Coating:

- 2 tablespoons cornflour
- 2 tablespoons all-purpose flour (maida)
- 1/2 teaspoon red chili powder
- Salt to taste

For Frying:

- Oil for deep frying

For Seasoning:

- Curry leaves (optional)
- Green chilies, slit
- 1 tablespoon garlic, finely chopped
- 1 tablespoon ginger, finely chopped

For Garnish:

- Fresh coriander leaves, chopped
- Lemon wedges

Instructions:

Marinating the Chicken:
- In a bowl, mix together yogurt, ginger-garlic paste, red chili powder, turmeric powder, garam masala, cornflour, all-purpose flour, salt, and lemon juice to make a smooth marinade.
- Add the chicken pieces to the marinade, ensuring they are well coated. Marinate for at least 2 hours or overnight in the refrigerator.

Coating the Chicken:
- In a separate bowl, mix cornflour, all-purpose flour, red chili powder, and salt to create a coating mixture.
- Toss the marinated chicken pieces in the coating mixture until they are evenly coated.

Deep Frying:
- Heat oil in a deep fryer or a heavy-bottomed pan to 350°F (175°C).
- Deep-fry the coated chicken pieces in batches until they are golden brown and cooked through. Drain on paper towels.

Seasoning:
- In a separate pan, heat a little oil. Add curry leaves (if using), slit green chilies, finely chopped garlic, and finely chopped ginger.
- Sauté for a minute until the garlic turns golden brown.

Tossing the Chicken:
- Add the fried chicken pieces to the seasoning mixture. Toss well to coat the chicken with the seasoning.

Garnish:
- Garnish with chopped coriander leaves and serve hot with lemon wedges on the side.

Chicken 65 is best enjoyed as a starter or appetizer with mint chutney or your favorite dipping sauce. It's a flavorful and spicy dish that is sure to be a hit at any gathering.

Sambar

Ingredients:

For Marination:

- 500g boneless chicken, cut into bite-sized pieces
- 1 cup thick yogurt
- 1 tablespoon ginger-garlic paste
- 1 teaspoon red chili powder
- 1/2 teaspoon turmeric powder
- 1 teaspoon garam masala
- 1 teaspoon cumin powder
- 1 teaspoon coriander powder
- 1 tablespoon lemon juice
- Salt to taste
- 2 tablespoons cornflour or rice flour

For Frying:

- Oil for deep frying

For Tempering:

- 2 tablespoons oil
- 1 tablespoon finely chopped garlic
- 1 tablespoon finely chopped ginger
- 2-3 green chilies, slit
- Curry leaves

For Garnish:

- Chopped coriander leaves
- Lemon wedges

Instructions:

Marination:

- In a bowl, combine yogurt, ginger-garlic paste, red chili powder, turmeric powder, garam masala, cumin powder, coriander powder, lemon juice, salt, and cornflour or rice flour. Mix well to form a thick marinade.
- Add the chicken pieces to the marinade, ensuring they are well-coated. Marinate for at least 2 hours, or preferably overnight for the best flavor.

Frying:
- Heat oil in a deep frying pan over medium heat.
- Once the oil is hot, deep fry the marinated chicken pieces until they are golden brown and crispy. Fry in batches if necessary.
- Remove the fried chicken pieces and place them on a plate lined with paper towels to absorb excess oil.

Tempering:
- In a separate pan, heat 2 tablespoons of oil.
- Add finely chopped garlic and ginger. Sauté until they become golden brown.
- Add slit green chilies and curry leaves. Sauté for a minute.

Final Toss:
- Add the fried chicken pieces to the tempering mixture.
- Toss the chicken in the tempering mixture, ensuring the pieces are well-coated and infused with the flavors.

Garnish and Serve:
- Garnish with chopped coriander leaves and serve hot.
- Optionally, serve with lemon wedges on the side.

Chicken 65 is ready to be served as a delicious appetizer or snack. Enjoy the crispy and flavorful chicken bites!

Baingan Ka Bharta

Ingredients:

- 1 large eggplant (baingan/brinjal)
- 2 tablespoons oil
- 1 teaspoon cumin seeds
- 1 large onion, finely chopped
- 2 tomatoes, finely chopped
- 1 tablespoon ginger-garlic paste
- 2 green chilies, finely chopped (adjust to taste)
- 1 teaspoon turmeric powder
- 1 teaspoon red chili powder (adjust to taste)
- 1 teaspoon coriander powder
- 1/2 teaspoon garam masala
- Salt to taste
- Fresh coriander leaves for garnish

Instructions:

Roasting the Eggplant:
- Roast the eggplant directly over an open flame on a gas stove or on a grill until the skin is charred and the flesh is soft. Alternatively, you can roast it in an oven at 200°C (392°F) for about 30-40 minutes, turning occasionally.

Peeling and Mashing:
- Let the roasted eggplant cool. Peel off the charred skin and mash the flesh thoroughly. You can also finely chop it if you prefer a chunkier texture.

Cooking the Bharta:
- Heat oil in a pan. Add cumin seeds and let them splutter.
- Add finely chopped onions and sauté until they become translucent.

Adding Aromatics:
- Add ginger-garlic paste and green chilies. Sauté for a minute until the raw smell disappears.

Spice Powders:
- Add turmeric powder, red chili powder, coriander powder, and salt. Mix well and cook for a couple of minutes.

Tomatoes:
- Add finely chopped tomatoes and cook until they become soft and the oil starts to separate.

Adding Roasted Eggplant:

- Add the mashed or chopped roasted eggplant to the pan. Mix well with the masala and let it cook for 5-7 minutes, stirring occasionally.

Garam Masala and Garnish:

- Add garam masala and mix. Adjust salt and spices according to your taste.
- Garnish with fresh coriander leaves.

Serve:

- Baingan ka Bharta is ready to be served. It goes well with roti, naan, or rice.

Enjoy your flavorful Baingan ka Bharta!

Tandoori Fish

Ingredients:

- 1 large eggplant (baingan)
- 2 medium-sized tomatoes, finely chopped
- 1 large onion, finely chopped
- 2 green chilies, finely chopped (adjust to taste)
- 1 tablespoon ginger-garlic paste
- 1/2 teaspoon turmeric powder
- 1 teaspoon red chili powder (adjust to taste)
- 1 teaspoon coriander powder
- 1/2 teaspoon cumin powder
- Salt to taste
- 2 tablespoons oil
- Fresh coriander leaves for garnish

Instructions:

Roasting the Eggplant:
- Wash the eggplant and pat it dry. Apply a little oil on the surface of the eggplant.
- Roast the eggplant directly over an open flame or on a gas stove until the skin is charred and the inner flesh is soft. Alternatively, you can bake it in the oven at 200°C (392°F) for about 40-45 minutes.
- Let the roasted eggplant cool. Once cooled, peel off the charred skin and mash the flesh well.

Cooking the Bharta:
- Heat oil in a pan over medium heat. Add chopped onions and sauté until they become translucent.
- Add ginger-garlic paste and chopped green chilies. Sauté for another minute until the raw smell disappears.
- Add turmeric powder, red chili powder, coriander powder, cumin powder, and salt. Mix well and cook for a couple of minutes.
- Add chopped tomatoes and cook until they become soft and the oil starts to separate.
- Add the mashed roasted eggplant to the pan. Mix well with the spice mixture and cook for 5-7 minutes, stirring occasionally.

Garnish and Serve:
- Garnish Baingan Ka Bharta with fresh coriander leaves.
- Serve hot with roti, naan, or rice.

Enjoy your Baingan Ka Bharta, a flavorful and smoky Indian eggplant dish!

Now, for Tandoori Fish:

Ingredients:

- 500g fish fillets (boneless pieces)
- 1 cup thick yogurt
- 1 tablespoon ginger-garlic paste
- 1 teaspoon red chili powder (adjust to taste)
- 1 teaspoon turmeric powder
- 1 teaspoon cumin powder
- 1 teaspoon coriander powder
- 1 teaspoon garam masala
- Salt to taste
- 2 tablespoons lemon juice
- 2 tablespoons vegetable oil
- Fresh coriander leaves for garnish (optional)

Instructions:

Marination:
- In a bowl, combine yogurt, ginger-garlic paste, red chili powder, turmeric powder, cumin powder, coriander powder, garam masala, salt, lemon juice, and vegetable oil. Mix well to form a smooth marinade.

Marinating the Fish:
- Pat the fish fillets dry with a paper towel. Coat the fish fillets with the prepared marinade, ensuring they are well-covered. Marinate for at least 1-2 hours in the refrigerator.

Grilling/Baking:
- Preheat your grill or oven to a high temperature.

- If grilling, place the marinated fish fillets on the grill and cook for 10-15 minutes, turning occasionally, until the fish is cooked through and has a nice char.
- If baking, preheat your oven to 200°C (392°F) and bake the fish for 20-25 minutes or until it flakes easily with a fork.

Garnish and Serve:

- Garnish the Tandoori Fish with fresh coriander leaves (optional).
- Serve hot with mint chutney or your favorite sauce.

Enjoy your Tandoori Fish, a flavorful and spicy grilled fish dish!

Chicken Do Pyaza

Ingredients:

- 500g chicken, cut into pieces
- 2 large onions, thinly sliced
- 2 tomatoes, finely chopped
- 2 green chilies, finely chopped
- 1 tablespoon ginger-garlic paste
- 1/2 cup yogurt
- 1 teaspoon cumin seeds
- 1 teaspoon turmeric powder
- 1 teaspoon red chili powder (adjust to taste)
- 1 teaspoon coriander powder
- 1/2 teaspoon garam masala
- Salt to taste
- 2 tablespoons cooking oil or ghee
- Fresh coriander leaves for garnish

Instructions:

Marinating the Chicken:
- In a bowl, mix the chicken pieces with yogurt, ginger-garlic paste, turmeric powder, red chili powder, coriander powder, and salt. Allow it to marinate for at least 30 minutes.

Cooking the Chicken:
- Heat oil or ghee in a pan over medium heat. Add cumin seeds and let them splutter.
- Add thinly sliced onions and sauté until they become golden brown.
- Add green chilies and ginger-garlic paste. Sauté for a couple of minutes until the raw smell disappears.
- Add the marinated chicken to the pan. Cook until the chicken changes color and is seared on all sides.
- Add chopped tomatoes, turmeric powder, red chili powder, coriander powder, and salt. Mix well and cook until the tomatoes are soft and the oil starts to separate.
- Add garam masala and cook for an additional 2-3 minutes.

Double Onions:

- Add another sliced onion to the pan. This onion will remain slightly crunchy and add texture to the dish.
- Cook until the chicken is fully cooked, and the flavors are well combined.

Garnish and Serve:
- Garnish with fresh coriander leaves.
- Serve Chicken Do Pyaza hot with naan, roti, or steamed rice.

Enjoy the rich and aromatic Chicken Do Pyaza!

Gobi Manchurian

Ingredients:

For Gobi Fritters:

- 1 medium-sized cauliflower, cut into florets
- 1 cup all-purpose flour (maida)
- 1/4 cup cornflour
- 1 tablespoon ginger-garlic paste
- 1 teaspoon soy sauce
- 1 teaspoon red chili powder
- 1/2 teaspoon black pepper powder
- Salt to taste
- Water (as needed for the batter)
- Oil for deep frying

For Manchurian Sauce:

- 1 tablespoon oil
- 1 tablespoon finely chopped garlic
- 1 tablespoon finely chopped ginger
- 1/2 cup finely chopped onions
- 1/4 cup finely chopped bell peppers (optional)
- 2 tablespoons soy sauce
- 1 tablespoon tomato ketchup
- 1 tablespoon chili sauce (adjust to taste)
- 1 tablespoon vinegar
- 1 teaspoon sugar
- Salt to taste
- 1 tablespoon cornflour mixed with 3 tablespoons water (for thickening)
- Chopped green onions for garnish

Instructions:

For Gobi Fritters:

In a bowl, mix all-purpose flour, cornflour, ginger-garlic paste, soy sauce, red chili powder, black pepper powder, and salt.

Gradually add water to make a thick, smooth batter. The consistency should be thick enough to coat the cauliflower florets.
Dip each cauliflower floret into the batter, ensuring it is well-coated.
Heat oil in a deep frying pan over medium heat. Deep fry the cauliflower florets until they are golden brown and crispy. Remove and place them on a plate lined with paper towels to absorb excess oil.

For Manchurian Sauce:

In a separate pan, heat oil over medium heat. Add finely chopped garlic and ginger. Sauté for a minute until aromatic.
Add chopped onions and bell peppers (if using). Sauté until the onions become translucent.
Add soy sauce, tomato ketchup, chili sauce, vinegar, sugar, and salt. Mix well.
Stir in the cornflour-water mixture to thicken the sauce. Cook until the sauce reaches the desired consistency.
Add the fried cauliflower florets to the sauce. Toss them gently until each floret is coated in the Manchurian sauce.
Garnish with chopped green onions.

Serve Gobi Manchurian hot as an appetizer or as a side dish with fried rice or noodles. Enjoy your delicious Indo-Chinese treat!

Rajasthani Dal Baati

Ingredients:

For Baati:

- 2 cups whole wheat flour
- 1/2 cup semolina (sooji)
- 1/2 cup ghee (clarified butter)
- 1 teaspoon carom seeds (ajwain)
- Salt to taste
- Water (as needed to knead the dough)

For Dal (Lentil Curry):

- 1 cup split yellow moong dal
- 1/4 cup split pigeon peas (toor dal)
- 1/4 cup split black gram (urad dal)
- 1 teaspoon mustard seeds
- 1 teaspoon cumin seeds
- 1/2 teaspoon asafoetida (hing)
- 1 onion, finely chopped
- 1 tomato, chopped
- 1 tablespoon ginger-garlic paste
- 2 green chilies, chopped
- 1/2 teaspoon turmeric powder
- 1 teaspoon red chili powder (adjust to taste)
- 1 teaspoon coriander powder
- 1 teaspoon garam masala
- Salt to taste
- 2 tablespoons ghee (clarified butter)
- Fresh coriander leaves for garnish

Instructions:

For Baati:

In a mixing bowl, combine whole wheat flour, semolina, ghee, carom seeds, and salt.
Gradually add water and knead the ingredients into a firm dough.

Divide the dough into small portions and shape them into round balls.
Preheat your oven to 180°C (356°F). Place the baati balls on a baking sheet and bake for about 30-40 minutes or until they are golden brown and cooked through.
Alternatively, you can roast the baatis on an open flame until they are evenly cooked from all sides. Keep turning them to ensure uniform roasting.
Once the baatis are done, brush them with ghee for added flavor.

For Dal:

Rinse the moong dal, toor dal, and urad dal together. Cook them in a pressure cooker with enough water until they are soft and mushy.
In a separate pan, heat ghee. Add mustard seeds and cumin seeds. Allow them to splutter.
Add asafoetida, chopped onions, ginger-garlic paste, and green chilies. Sauté until the onions become golden brown.
Add chopped tomatoes and cook until they are soft.
Add turmeric powder, red chili powder, coriander powder, garam masala, and salt. Mix well.
Add the cooked lentils to the pan and bring the mixture to a boil. Adjust the consistency by adding water if needed.
Garnish with fresh coriander leaves.

Serve the hot Dal with Baati. Break the baatis into pieces and soak them in the dal before eating. Enjoy the authentic flavors of Rajasthani Dal Baati!

Chole Bhature

For Chole (Spicy Chickpeas):

Ingredients:

- 1 cup dried chickpeas, soaked overnight (or use canned chickpeas)
- 1 large onion, finely chopped
- 2 tomatoes, finely chopped
- 2 green chilies, slit
- 1 tablespoon ginger-garlic paste
- 1 teaspoon cumin seeds
- 1 teaspoon coriander powder
- 1/2 teaspoon turmeric powder
- 1 teaspoon red chili powder (adjust to taste)
- 1 teaspoon garam masala
- 1 teaspoon dried mango powder (amchur)
- Salt to taste
- Fresh coriander leaves for garnish
- 2 tablespoons cooking oil

Instructions:

Cooking the Chickpeas:
- If using dried chickpeas, rinse and soak them overnight. Pressure cook the soaked chickpeas until they are soft and cooked through. If using canned chickpeas, drain and rinse them.

Making the Chole:
- Heat oil in a pan. Add cumin seeds and let them splutter.
- Add chopped onions and sauté until they become golden brown.
- Add ginger-garlic paste and slit green chilies. Sauté for a minute until the raw smell disappears.
- Add chopped tomatoes and cook until they become soft and the oil starts to separate.
- Add coriander powder, turmeric powder, red chili powder, garam masala, dried mango powder, and salt. Mix well and cook for a couple of minutes.
- Add the cooked chickpeas and mix them with the spice mixture. Allow it to simmer for 10-15 minutes, allowing the flavors to meld.

- Garnish with fresh coriander leaves.

For Bhature (Fried Bread):

Ingredients:

- 2 cups all-purpose flour (maida)
- 1/2 cup semolina (sooji)
- 1/2 cup yogurt
- 1/2 teaspoon baking soda
- 1/2 teaspoon sugar
- Salt to taste
- Water (as needed to knead the dough)
- Oil for deep frying

Instructions:

Making the Dough:
- In a large bowl, combine all-purpose flour, semolina, yogurt, baking soda, sugar, and salt.
- Gradually add water and knead the ingredients into a soft and smooth dough. Cover the dough with a damp cloth and let it rest for at least 2 hours.

Making Bhature:
- Divide the dough into small portions and roll them into balls.
- Roll each ball into a flat, oval-shaped bhatura using a rolling pin.
- Heat oil in a deep frying pan. Carefully slide the rolled bhatura into the hot oil.
- Fry until the bhatura puffs up and becomes golden brown on both sides.
- Remove the bhatura from the oil and place it on a paper towel to absorb excess oil.

Serve Chole Bhature:

- Serve hot Chole with Bhature.
- Garnish with additional fresh coriander leaves and sliced onions.
- Optionally, serve with pickles or yogurt on the side.

Enjoy your delicious and indulgent Chole Bhature!

Chicken Chettinad

Ingredients:

For Marination:

- 500g chicken, cleaned and cut into pieces
- 1 cup thick yogurt
- 1 teaspoon turmeric powder
- 1 teaspoon red chili powder
- Salt to taste

For Chettinad Masala:

- 2 tablespoons oil
- 1 tablespoon coriander seeds
- 1 teaspoon cumin seeds
- 1 teaspoon fennel seeds
- 1/2 teaspoon black peppercorns
- 4-5 dry red chilies (adjust to taste)
- 1-inch cinnamon stick
- 3-4 green cardamom pods
- 3-4 cloves
- 2-3 curry leaves

For Chicken Chettinad Curry:

- 2 tablespoons oil
- 1 large onion, finely chopped
- 1 tablespoon ginger-garlic paste
- 2 tomatoes, finely chopped
- 1/2 cup coconut milk (optional)
- Salt to taste
- Fresh coriander leaves for garnish

Instructions:

Marination:

In a bowl, mix the chicken pieces with yogurt, turmeric powder, red chili powder, and salt. Marinate for at least 30 minutes.

Chettinad Masala:

Heat 2 tablespoons of oil in a pan. Add coriander seeds, cumin seeds, fennel seeds, black peppercorns, dry red chilies, cinnamon stick, green cardamom pods, cloves, and curry leaves.
Roast the spices over medium heat until they become fragrant. Be careful not to burn them.
Allow the roasted spices to cool, and then grind them into a fine powder. This is your Chettinad masala.

Chicken Chettinad Curry:

Heat 2 tablespoons of oil in a pan. Add finely chopped onions and sauté until they become golden brown.
Add ginger-garlic paste and sauté for a minute until the raw smell disappears.
Add finely chopped tomatoes and cook until they become soft and the oil starts to separate.
Add the marinated chicken and cook until the chicken is browned.
Add the freshly ground Chettinad masala and mix well.
Pour in coconut milk (if using) and cook for another 10-15 minutes until the chicken is cooked through, and the curry reaches the desired consistency.
Adjust salt and garnish with fresh coriander leaves.

Serve Chicken Chettinad with steamed rice, dosa, or idli for a delicious South Indian

meal. Enjoy the bold and spicy flavors of this traditional dish!

Kathi Roll

Ingredients:

For Chicken Marinade:

- 500g boneless chicken, thinly sliced
- 1 cup yogurt
- 1 tablespoon ginger-garlic paste
- 1 teaspoon red chili powder
- 1/2 teaspoon turmeric powder
- 1 teaspoon garam masala
- Salt to taste
- 2 tablespoons oil
- Skewers for grilling

For Filling:

- 1 large onion, thinly sliced
- 1 bell pepper, thinly sliced
- 2 tablespoons oil
- 1 teaspoon cumin seeds
- 1 teaspoon ginger-garlic paste
- 1 teaspoon chaat masala
- 1 teaspoon roasted cumin powder
- Salt to taste
- Fresh coriander leaves for garnish

For Paratha:

- Ready-made parathas or make your own with whole wheat flour
- Butter or oil for cooking parathas

Instructions:

Marinating the Chicken:

In a bowl, mix yogurt, ginger-garlic paste, red chili powder, turmeric powder, garam masala, salt, and oil.

Add the sliced chicken to the marinade, ensuring it is well-coated. Marinate for at least 1-2 hours or overnight in the refrigerator.
Thread the marinated chicken onto skewers.
Grill the chicken skewers until they are cooked through and have a nice char on the surface. You can also cook the chicken in an oven or on a stovetop grilling pan.

Preparing the Filling:

Heat oil in a pan. Add cumin seeds and let them splutter.
Add thinly sliced onions and sauté until they become golden brown.
Add ginger-garlic paste and cook for a minute until the raw smell disappears.
Add thinly sliced bell peppers and sauté for a couple of minutes until they are slightly tender but still crisp.
Add chaat masala, roasted cumin powder, and salt. Mix well.
Add the grilled chicken pieces to the pan and toss everything together. Cook for a few more minutes until the flavors meld.

Assembling the Kathi Roll:

Heat the parathas according to the package instructions or cook your own parathas.
Place a portion of the prepared chicken filling in the center of a paratha.
Garnish with fresh coriander leaves.
Roll the paratha tightly, securing the filling inside.
Wrap the bottom half of the roll with a piece of parchment paper or foil to make it easier to hold and eat.

Serve the Chicken Kathi Roll immediately. You can also add a drizzle of mint chutney or your favorite sauce for extra flavor. Enjoy this delicious and convenient street food!

Chicken Sukka

Kathi Roll:

For Chicken Filling:

Ingredients:

- 500g boneless chicken, thinly sliced
- 2 tablespoons yogurt
- 1 tablespoon ginger-garlic paste
- 1 teaspoon red chili powder
- 1/2 teaspoon turmeric powder
- 1 teaspoon garam masala
- Salt to taste
- 2 tablespoons oil
- Sliced onions, bell peppers, and tomatoes (for filling)
- Fresh coriander leaves (for garnish)

Instructions:

In a bowl, marinate the chicken slices with yogurt, ginger-garlic paste, red chili powder, turmeric powder, garam masala, and salt. Let it marinate for at least 30 minutes.
Heat oil in a pan over medium heat. Add the marinated chicken and cook until it's tender and cooked through.
In the same pan, add sliced onions, bell peppers, and tomatoes. Sauté until they are slightly cooked but still retain their crunch.
Warm the rotis or parathas, and place a portion of the cooked chicken mixture in the center.
Garnish with fresh coriander leaves.
Roll the paratha tightly to form a Kathi Roll. Serve hot.

Chicken Sukka:

Ingredients:

- 500g chicken, cut into small pieces
- 1 cup grated coconut
- 1 large onion, finely chopped
- 2 tomatoes, finely chopped
- 2 tablespoons oil
- 1 teaspoon mustard seeds
- 1 teaspoon cumin seeds
- 1 sprig curry leaves
- 1 tablespoon ginger-garlic paste
- 2 tablespoons red chili powder (adjust to taste)
- 1 tablespoon coriander powder
- 1/2 teaspoon turmeric powder
- Salt to taste
- Fresh coriander leaves (for garnish)

Instructions:

Dry roast the grated coconut until it turns golden brown. Set it aside.
Heat oil in a pan. Add mustard seeds, cumin seeds, and curry leaves. Allow them to splutter.
Add chopped onions and sauté until they become golden brown.
Add ginger-garlic paste and sauté for a minute until the raw smell disappears.
Add chopped tomatoes and cook until they become soft and the oil starts to separate.
Add red chili powder, coriander powder, turmeric powder, and salt. Mix well.
Add the chicken pieces and cook until they are well coated with the spices.
Add the roasted coconut and mix well. Cook until the chicken is tender and the mixture is dry.
Garnish with fresh coriander leaves.

Serve Chicken Sukka with rice or Indian bread. Enjoy the rich and spicy flavors!

Mutton Curry

Ingredients:

- 500g mutton, cut into pieces
- 2 large onions, finely chopped
- 2 tomatoes, finely chopped
- 1/4 cup oil or ghee
- 1 tablespoon ginger-garlic paste
- 2 tablespoons yogurt
- 1 teaspoon turmeric powder
- 1 tablespoon red chili powder (adjust to taste)
- 1 tablespoon coriander powder
- 1/2 teaspoon cumin powder
- 1 teaspoon garam masala
- Salt to taste
- Fresh coriander leaves for garnish

Whole Spices:

- 2 bay leaves
- 4-5 green cardamom pods
- 4-5 cloves
- 1-inch cinnamon stick
- 1 teaspoon cumin seeds

Instructions:

Marinating the Mutton:
- In a bowl, mix the mutton pieces with yogurt, turmeric powder, red chili powder, coriander powder, cumin powder, and salt. Allow it to marinate for at least 1 hour.

Cooking the Mutton:
- Heat oil or ghee in a pressure cooker or a heavy-bottomed pan.
- Add bay leaves, green cardamom pods, cloves, cinnamon stick, and cumin seeds. Sauté until they release their aroma.
- Add chopped onions and sauté until they become golden brown.
- Add ginger-garlic paste and sauté for a minute until the raw smell disappears.

- Add chopped tomatoes and cook until they become soft and the oil starts to separate.
- Add the marinated mutton and cook until it's browned on all sides.
- Add garam masala and mix well.
- If using a pressure cooker, add about 1-2 cups of water, depending on the desired consistency. Close the lid and cook for 4-5 whistles or until the mutton is tender. If using a pan, add enough water to cover the mutton, then cover and simmer until the mutton is tender.

Final Touch:
- Once the mutton is cooked, adjust the seasoning and consistency according to your preference.
- Garnish with fresh coriander leaves.

Serve Mutton Curry hot with steamed rice, naan, or roti. Enjoy the rich and flavorful mutton curry!

Tomato Rasam

Ingredients:

- 3 large tomatoes, chopped
- 1 small lemon-sized tamarind ball (soaked in warm water)
- 1/2 cup cooked toor dal (pigeon pea lentils)
- 1 teaspoon cumin seeds
- 1 teaspoon black pepper
- 2-3 green chilies, chopped
- 1-inch piece of ginger, grated
- 1/2 teaspoon mustard seeds
- 1/2 teaspoon turmeric powder
- A pinch of asafoetida (hing)
- 1 sprig curry leaves
- 2 tablespoons chopped coriander leaves
- 1 tablespoon ghee or oil
- Salt to taste

For Tempering:

- 1 tablespoon ghee or oil
- 1/2 teaspoon mustard seeds
- 1/2 teaspoon cumin seeds
- 2-3 dry red chilies
- A pinch of asafoetida (hing)

Instructions:

Preparing Tamarind Extract:
- Soak the tamarind in warm water for about 15 minutes. Squeeze it to extract the tamarind juice, and discard the pulp.

Making Tomato Rasam:
- In a blender, grind chopped tomatoes, cumin seeds, black pepper, green chilies, and grated ginger into a smooth paste.
- In a pot, combine the tomato paste, tamarind extract, cooked toor dal, turmeric powder, mustard seeds, asafoetida, curry leaves, and salt. Add enough water to achieve the desired consistency.
- Bring the mixture to a boil and simmer for 10-15 minutes on medium heat.

Tempering (Tadka):
- In a small pan, heat ghee or oil for tempering.
- Add mustard seeds, cumin seeds, dry red chilies, and a pinch of asafoetida. Allow the mustard seeds to splutter.
- Pour the tempering over the rasam and mix well.

Garnish:
- Garnish the rasam with chopped coriander leaves.

Serve:
- Serve Tomato Rasam hot with steamed rice. It can also be enjoyed as a soup or with idli or dosa.

Enjoy this comforting and tangy Tomato Rasam!

Dosa

Ingredients:

For Dosa Batter:

- 1 cup parboiled rice
- 1 cup regular rice
- 1/2 cup urad dal (black gram)
- 1/4 teaspoon fenugreek seeds
- Water (for soaking and grinding)
- Salt to taste

For Making Dosas:

- Dosa batter
- Oil or ghee (for cooking)

Instructions:

Preparing Dosa Batter:

Soaking:
- Rinse the parboiled rice, regular rice, urad dal, and fenugreek seeds together in plenty of water. Soak them in water for at least 6-8 hours or overnight.

Grinding:
- Drain the soaked ingredients and grind them into a smooth batter using a wet grinder or a blender. Add water gradually as needed during grinding.
- The consistency of the batter should be like pancake batter. It should not be too thick or too thin.
- Add salt to the batter and mix well.

Fermentation:
- Transfer the batter to a large bowl. Cover it with a lid and let it ferment in a warm place for about 8-12 hours or until it doubles in volume.
- The fermented batter should have a slight sour aroma.

Making Dosas:

Heat the Griddle (Tawa):

- Heat a non-stick or cast-iron griddle (tawa) on medium-high heat.

Greasing the Griddle:

- If using a cast-iron griddle, lightly grease it with oil.
- If using a non-stick griddle, no greasing is usually required.

Pouring the Batter:

- Take a ladleful of the fermented dosa batter and pour it onto the center of the hot griddle.

Spreading the Batter:

- Using the back of the ladle or a circular motion of the ladle, spread the batter in a thin, even layer to form a round dosa.

Drizzling Oil or Ghee:

- Drizzle a little oil or ghee around the edges of the dosa.

Cooking:

- Cook the dosa on medium-high heat until the edges start to lift and become crisp, and the bottom turns golden brown.

Folding:

- You can fold the dosa in half or roll it into a cylinder as per your preference.

Serve:

- Remove the dosa from the griddle and repeat the process with the remaining batter.

Serve Dosas hot with coconut chutney, sambar, or your favorite curry. Enjoy this classic South Indian delicacy!

Achari Chicken

Dosa:

Ingredients:

For Dosa Batter:

- 2 cups parboiled rice
- 1/2 cup urad dal (split black gram)
- 1/2 teaspoon fenugreek seeds
- Salt to taste
- Water (as needed for grinding)

For Making Dosas:

- Oil or ghee (for cooking)
- Potato masala or any desired filling (optional)

Instructions:

Making Dosa Batter:

Wash the parboiled rice, urad dal, and fenugreek seeds together.
Soak them in water for at least 4-6 hours.
Grind the soaked ingredients into a smooth batter. Add water as needed to achieve a slightly thick consistency.
Add salt to the batter and mix well. Allow the batter to ferment overnight or for at least 8 hours.

Making Dosas:

Heat a flat griddle or non-stick pan.
Pour a ladleful of dosa batter onto the center of the hot griddle and spread it in a circular motion to form a thin, even layer.
Drizzle some oil or ghee around the edges of the dosa.
Cook until the edges start to lift and the underside becomes golden brown.

Optionally, flip the dosa and cook the other side for a brief moment. Remove the dosa from the griddle and repeat the process for the remaining batter.
Serve hot dosas with coconut chutney, sambar, or any desired filling.

Achari Chicken:

Ingredients:

- 500g chicken, cut into pieces
- 2 tablespoons oil
- 1 teaspoon mustard seeds
- 1 teaspoon cumin seeds
- 1 teaspoon fennel seeds
- 1/2 teaspoon fenugreek seeds
- 1 large onion, finely chopped
- 1 tablespoon ginger-garlic paste
- 2 tomatoes, finely chopped
- 1/2 cup yogurt
- 1 teaspoon turmeric powder
- 1 tablespoon red chili powder (adjust to taste)
- 1 tablespoon coriander powder
- 1/2 teaspoon cumin powder
- 1/2 teaspoon garam masala
- Salt to taste
- Fresh coriander leaves for garnish

Instructions:

Heat oil in a pan. Add mustard seeds, cumin seeds, fennel seeds, and fenugreek seeds. Let them splutter.
Add finely chopped onions and sauté until they become golden brown.
Add ginger-garlic paste and sauté for a minute until the raw smell disappears.
Add finely chopped tomatoes and cook until they become soft and the oil starts to separate.
Add turmeric powder, red chili powder, coriander powder, cumin powder, and salt. Mix well and cook for a couple of minutes.
Add the chicken pieces to the pan and cook until they are browned.
Add yogurt and garam masala. Mix well and cook until the chicken is tender and the flavors are well combined.
Garnish with fresh coriander leaves.

Serve Achari Chicken with hot dosas, rice, or Indian bread. Enjoy the delicious and tangy flavors of Achari Chicken!

Kheema Pav

Ingredients:

For Kheema (Minced Meat):

- 500g minced meat (chicken, lamb, or beef)
- 2 tablespoons oil
- 1 large onion, finely chopped
- 1 tablespoon ginger-garlic paste
- 2 tomatoes, finely chopped
- 2 green chilies, finely chopped
- 1/2 cup peas (optional)
- 1 teaspoon red chili powder (adjust to taste)
- 1/2 teaspoon turmeric powder
- 1 teaspoon garam masala
- Salt to taste
- Fresh coriander leaves for garnish

For Pav:

- Soft pav/bread rolls

Instructions:

Making Kheema:

Heat oil in a pan. Add finely chopped onions and sauté until they become golden brown.
Add ginger-garlic paste and sauté for a minute until the raw smell disappears.
Add finely chopped tomatoes and green chilies. Cook until the tomatoes are soft and the oil starts to separate.
Add minced meat and cook until it's browned.
Add red chili powder, turmeric powder, garam masala, and salt. Mix well and cook for a few minutes until the spices are well incorporated.
If using peas, add them to the kheema and cook until they are tender.
Garnish with fresh coriander leaves.

Serving with Pav:

Heat the pav/bread rolls on a griddle or in the oven until they are warm.

Slice the pav horizontally without cutting through completely.
Spoon the prepared kheema into the sliced pav.
Optionally, serve with a slice of lime and chopped onions on the side.
Garnish with additional coriander leaves.
Serve Kheema Pav hot and enjoy the delicious street food flavors.

Kheema Pav is often served with a side of lime wedges, chopped onions, and green chutney. It's a flavorful and satisfying dish that you can enjoy for breakfast, lunch, or dinner.

Chicken Handi

Ingredients:

- 500g chicken, cut into pieces
- 2 tablespoons oil or ghee
- 1 large onion, finely chopped
- 1 tablespoon ginger-garlic paste
- 2 tomatoes, finely chopped
- 1/2 cup yogurt
- 1 teaspoon turmeric powder
- 1 tablespoon red chili powder (adjust to taste)
- 1 tablespoon coriander powder
- 1/2 teaspoon cumin powder
- 1 teaspoon garam masala
- Salt to taste
- 1/2 cup cream (optional)
- Fresh coriander leaves for garnish

Instructions:

Heat oil or ghee in a handi or a deep, heavy-bottomed pan.
Add finely chopped onions and sauté until they become golden brown.
Add ginger-garlic paste and sauté for a minute until the raw smell disappears.
Add finely chopped tomatoes and cook until they become soft and the oil starts to separate.
Add chicken pieces to the pan and cook until they are browned.
In a bowl, whisk yogurt and add it to the pan. Stir continuously to avoid curdling.
Add turmeric powder, red chili powder, coriander powder, cumin powder, garam masala, and salt. Mix well and cook for a few minutes until the spices are well incorporated.
If using cream, add it to the pan and mix well. This adds richness to the dish.
Cook the chicken until it's tender and the gravy reaches the desired consistency.
Garnish with fresh coriander leaves.
Serve Chicken Handi hot with naan, roti, or steamed rice.

Enjoy the rich and creamy flavors of Chicken Handi!

Bhel Puri

Ingredients:

- 4 cups puffed rice (murmura)
- 1 cup sev (crispy chickpea noodles)
- 1 cup boiled potatoes, diced
- 1/2 cup finely chopped onions
- 1/2 cup finely chopped tomatoes
- 1/4 cup finely chopped cucumber
- 1/4 cup roasted peanuts
- 2 tablespoons finely chopped coriander leaves
- 2 tablespoons tamarind chutney
- 2 tablespoons green chutney
- 1 teaspoon chaat masala
- 1/2 teaspoon roasted cumin powder
- 1/2 teaspoon red chili powder (adjust to taste)
- Salt to taste
- Lemon wedges for serving

Instructions:

In a large mixing bowl, combine puffed rice, sev, diced boiled potatoes, chopped onions, tomatoes, cucumber, roasted peanuts, and coriander leaves.
Add tamarind chutney and green chutney according to your taste preferences.
Adjust the quantity of chutneys for sweetness and spiciness.
Sprinkle chaat masala, roasted cumin powder, red chili powder, and salt over the mixture.
Toss the ingredients gently to combine everything well.
Serve Bhel Puri immediately in individual bowls or plates.
Garnish with additional sev and coriander leaves.
Squeeze fresh lemon juice over the Bhel Puri just before serving for an extra burst of flavor.
Enjoy this delicious and crunchy street food snack!

Bhel Puri is a versatile dish, and you can adjust the ingredients and chutneys according to your taste preferences. It's a perfect blend of textures and flavors, making it a popular choice for a quick and tasty snack.

Methi Chicken

Bhel Puri:

Ingredients:

- 2 cups puffed rice (murmura)
- 1 cup sev (thin gram flour noodles)
- 1 cup chopped tomatoes
- 1 cup boiled and chopped potatoes
- 1/2 cup chopped onions
- 1/2 cup chopped cucumber
- 1/4 cup chopped coriander leaves
- 2 tablespoons tamarind chutney
- 1 tablespoon green chutney
- 1 teaspoon chaat masala
- 1/2 teaspoon roasted cumin powder
- Salt to taste
- A pinch of red chili powder (optional)
- Pomegranate seeds for garnish (optional)
- Lemon wedges for serving

Instructions:

In a large mixing bowl, combine puffed rice, sev, chopped tomatoes, boiled potatoes, onions, cucumber, and coriander leaves.
Add tamarind chutney and green chutney according to your taste preferences.
Sprinkle chaat masala, roasted cumin powder, salt, and red chili powder (if using). Mix everything well.
Garnish with pomegranate seeds for a burst of sweetness.
Serve Bhel Puri immediately in bowls, garnished with additional coriander leaves, and with lemon wedges on the side.

Enjoy the crunchy and flavorful Bhel Puri!

Methi Chicken:

Ingredients:

- 500g chicken, cut into pieces
- 1 cup fresh fenugreek leaves (methi), washed and chopped
- 2 onions, finely chopped
- 2 tomatoes, finely chopped
- 1 tablespoon ginger-garlic paste
- 1/2 cup yogurt
- 1 teaspoon turmeric powder
- 1 tablespoon red chili powder (adjust to taste)
- 1 tablespoon coriander powder
- 1/2 teaspoon cumin powder
- 1 teaspoon garam masala
- Salt to taste
- 2 tablespoons oil
- Fresh coriander leaves for garnish

Instructions:

Heat oil in a pan. Add chopped onions and sauté until they become golden brown.
Add ginger-garlic paste and sauté for a minute until the raw smell disappears.
Add chopped tomatoes and cook until they become soft and the oil starts to separate.
Add chicken pieces to the pan and cook until they are browned.
Add turmeric powder, red chili powder, coriander powder, cumin powder, and salt. Mix well.
Stir in yogurt and chopped fenugreek leaves. Mix well and cook for a few minutes.
Cook until the chicken is tender, and the masala coats the pieces.
Add garam masala and garnish with fresh coriander leaves.
Serve Methi Chicken hot with naan, roti, or steamed rice.

Enjoy the aromatic and flavorful Methi Chicken!

Kadhi Pakora

For Pakoras (Gram Flour Dumplings):

Ingredients:

- 1 cup gram flour (besan)
- 1/2 cup finely chopped onions
- 1/4 cup finely chopped spinach (optional)
- 1/2 teaspoon red chili powder
- 1/2 teaspoon turmeric powder
- Salt to taste
- Water (as needed)
- Oil for deep frying

Instructions:

In a bowl, mix gram flour, chopped onions, chopped spinach, red chili powder, turmeric powder, and salt.
Add water gradually to make a thick batter. Ensure there are no lumps.
Heat oil in a deep frying pan. Drop spoonfuls of the batter into the hot oil and deep fry until the pakoras are golden brown and crispy.
Remove the pakoras from the oil and place them on a paper towel to absorb excess oil.

For Kadhi:

Ingredients:

- 1 cup yogurt, whisked
- 2 tablespoons gram flour (besan)
- 1 tablespoon oil or ghee
- 1 teaspoon mustard seeds
- 1 teaspoon cumin seeds
- 1/2 teaspoon fenugreek seeds
- 1/2 teaspoon asafoetida (hing)
- 1 onion, thinly sliced
- 1 tablespoon ginger-garlic paste
- 2 green chilies, slit
- 1/2 teaspoon turmeric powder

- 1 teaspoon red chili powder
- Salt to taste
- 2 cups water
- Fresh coriander leaves for garnish

Instructions:

In a bowl, whisk yogurt and gram flour together until smooth.
Heat oil or ghee in a pot. Add mustard seeds, cumin seeds, fenugreek seeds, and asafoetida. Let them splutter.
Add thinly sliced onions and sauté until they become golden brown.
Add ginger-garlic paste and green chilies. Sauté for a minute until the raw smell disappears.
Pour in the yogurt and gram flour mixture. Stir continuously to avoid lumps.
Add turmeric powder, red chili powder, and salt. Mix well.
Gradually add water while stirring continuously. Bring the mixture to a boil.
Simmer the kadhi on low heat for 15-20 minutes, stirring occasionally, until it thickens.
Add the fried pakoras to the kadhi and let it simmer for another 10 minutes.
Garnish with fresh coriander leaves.

Serve Kadhi Pakora hot with steamed rice or chapati. Enjoy the delightful combination of the tangy yogurt-based curry and the crispy gram flour dumplings!

Prawn Curry

Kadhi Pakora:

Ingredients:

For Kadhi:

- 1 cup gram flour (besan)
- 1 cup yogurt (whisked)
- 4 cups water
- 1 teaspoon mustard seeds
- 1/2 teaspoon fenugreek seeds
- 1/2 teaspoon cumin seeds
- 1/2 teaspoon turmeric powder
- 1/2 teaspoon red chili powder
- 2 tablespoons oil
- A pinch of asafoetida (hing)
- Salt to taste
- Fresh coriander leaves for garnish

For Pakoras:

- 1 cup gram flour (besan)
- 1 onion, finely chopped
- 1/2 cup spinach, chopped (optional)
- 1/2 teaspoon turmeric powder
- 1/2 teaspoon red chili powder
- Salt to taste
- Water (as needed for batter)
- Oil for deep frying

Instructions:

For Kadhi:

In a bowl, mix gram flour and whisked yogurt to form a smooth paste.
Heat oil in a pan, add mustard seeds, fenugreek seeds, and cumin seeds. Allow them to splutter.
Add asafoetida, turmeric powder, and red chili powder. Stir for a minute.

Pour the gram flour and yogurt mixture into the pan while continuously stirring to avoid lumps.
Add water gradually, stirring continuously to maintain a smooth consistency.
Let it simmer on low heat for 20-25 minutes, stirring occasionally.
Season with salt and garnish with fresh coriander leaves.

For Pakoras:

In a bowl, mix gram flour, chopped onions, chopped spinach (if using), turmeric powder, red chili powder, and salt.
Add water gradually to make a thick batter.
Heat oil in a deep frying pan.
Drop spoonfuls of the batter into the hot oil and fry until golden brown.
Remove the pakoras and drain excess oil on a paper towel.

Assembling Kadhi Pakora:

Add the fried pakoras to the simmering kadhi.
Let it cook for an additional 10-15 minutes.
Garnish with fresh coriander leaves.
Serve hot with steamed rice or chapati.

Prawn Curry:

Ingredients:

- 500g prawns, cleaned and deveined
- 2 tablespoons oil
- 1 onion, finely chopped
- 1 tablespoon ginger-garlic paste
- 2 tomatoes, finely chopped
- 1/2 cup coconut milk
- 1 teaspoon turmeric powder
- 1 tablespoon red chili powder (adjust to taste)
- 1 tablespoon coriander powder
- 1/2 teaspoon cumin powder
- 1 teaspoon garam masala
- Salt to taste
- Fresh coriander leaves for garnish

Instructions:

Heat oil in a pan. Add chopped onions and sauté until they become golden brown.
Add ginger-garlic paste and sauté for a minute until the raw smell disappears.
Add chopped tomatoes and cook until they become soft.
Add turmeric powder, red chili powder, coriander powder, cumin powder, and salt. Mix well and cook for a few minutes.
Add cleaned prawns to the pan and cook until they turn pink and opaque.
Pour in coconut milk and garam masala. Stir well.
Let it simmer for 5-7 minutes until the prawns are cooked through.
Garnish with fresh coriander leaves.
Serve the Prawn Curry hot with steamed rice or naan.

Enjoy your delicious Kadhi Pakora and Prawn Curry!

www.ingramcontent.com/pod-product-compliance
Lightning Source LLC
Chambersburg PA
CBHW060605120726
48002CB00010B/2829